POWERS OF THE SIXTH SENSE

HOW TO REMAIN SAFE IN A HOSTILE WORLD

First published by O-Books, 2008
O-Books is an imprint of John Hunt Publishing Ltd., Laurel House, Station Approach,
Alresford, Hants, SO24 9JH, UK
office1@o-books.net
www.o-books.com

For distributor details and how to order please visit the 'Ordering' section on our website.

Design: Stuart Davies

Printed in the UK by CPI Group (UK) Ltd, Croydon, CR0 4YY

We operate a distinctive and ethical publishing philosophy in all
areas of our business, from our global network of authors to
production and worldwide distribution.

POWERS OF THE SIXTH SENSE

HOW TO REMAIN SAFE IN A HOSTILE WORLD

By Jock Brocas

BOOKS

Winchester, UK
Washington, USA

Reading this book is a journey, and right from the beginning you get a sense of wonder as you grasp that the author is a person you can really learn from. Jock Brocas truly walks his talk, and from the first few pages I wanted to emulate him. This is no ordinary author. Only buy this book if you're as ready to become a pupil as he is to become a teacher. A genuine book for the modern day, combining readability, essential knowledge and a beautiful balance between spirituality and the reality of surviving in the physical world. Jenny Smedley, author of *Souls Don't Lie* and *Past life Angels*

"Powers of the Sixth Sense" is a compelling book that will inspire us all to develop and trust our psychic powers. Dr. Bruce Goldberg, author of *Custom Design Your Own Destiny*

Spiritual warrior meets Special Forces. A fascinating and practical guide to self-protection - using body and mind - in our increasingly dangerous world. This is a fascinating crossover book, combining practical self-defence tips with far more esoteric material about developing and using psychic abilities to stay safe. Accordingly, the author moves seamlessly from tried and tested martial arts techniques and counter-surveillance strategies, to intuition, mediumship and guardian angels. The sixth sense is a phrase one hears a lot. Some people believe that warnings of danger can be obtained through techniques such as ESP, while others think that feelings of unease about certain situations are caused by individuals subconsciously picking up on subtle clues relating to people's behaviour or to the environment. One could argue that the source doesn't matter - only the outcome. Perhaps it doesn't matter whether you label yourself perceptive, 'streetwise' or psychic: staying safe in this increasingly dangerous world is what's really important and this intriguing book will help you in this, whatever your beliefs. The author skilfully guides the reader through the art of becoming a spiritual warrior as well as a physical one. Nick Pope, MoD UFO Project, 1991 - 1994

This is a book you must read if you want the best skills for surviving safely. It is streetwise. It is unique in combining the expertise of self-defence, martial arts and psychic protection. From an experienced and practical teacher. William Bloom

This very practical book is written by a man with an unusual background and life experiences. Jock Brocas shares with us information and techniques to keep us safe that he has developed over years of training. This book is invaluable if you want to know how to keep secure at home and work, while travelling or socialising. In addition to very practical advice the author discusses the development of our intuition as a means to keeping us protected on all levels – physical, emotional, mental and spiritual. He covers positive thinking and intention, the aura, the benefits of meditation and provides exercises to train the sixth sense. Well worth a read and a handy book to refer back to at regular intervals. Sue Allen, author of *Spirit Release: A Practical Handbook.*

Jock Brocas brings a unique set of skills to the art and practise of psychic self-defence. The medium and spiritual warrior coalesce around a compassionate bodhisattva who seeks only to help the innocent protect themselves, their families and businesses from predators both physical and other-worldly. With candour, sensitivity and humour he lays to rest the shadowy world of diverse threats that slink and slither through our world, and his pointed advice will help many achieve peace of mind. Gordon Phinn, author of *Eternal Life And HowTo Enjoy It*

Jock provides insight into much that all we might ponder in life. He does so with experience and forethought, enabling you, the reader, to trust your feelings, intuition and instincts. Be alert – the world needs more alert individuals. Andrew Beattie, Australian Shihan 12th Dan Bujinkan

I thoroughly endorse this work by Jock Brocas who is a member and practitioner of the Bujinkan arts. The Bujinkan is an International Martial organisation headed by Japanese martial arts legend Dr Hatsumi who inherited this tradition from his teacher the legendary warrior Takamatsu Toshitsugu.

In our modern empirical world, the value of the subconscious is undervalued, yet it lies at the very heart of our innate survival sense. Rather than being something that is added to the practitioner, our system aims to cultivate this sense by years of training in natural movement. By this process the unnatural and inessential is stripped away and ability of the subconscious to naturally protect the person is freed and enabled. I thoroughly commend Jock Brocas for his efforts in bring this aspect of martial arts and life into the public awareness through his unique talents and experiences. In this sometimes troubled world I would recommend everyone to read this book and realise that your own mind and psyche have the ability to save your life in the most dire and severe circumstances. Peter King (Shi-Tenno) 15thS Dan Bujinkan

This book is exceptionally well written and has some unique perspectives on safety, especially being able to diffuse a situation while it occurs or before the event by using your natural intuitive ability. The way in which the author has integrated stories that people can use practically in their lives is excellent. This book is a lifeline for people and an important asset for the human race. Tacy S. Trump, Senior Executive Producer, VoiceAmerica

Jock Brocas' "Powers of the Sixth Sense" is a unique and compelling work dealing with the most important issue in our world today, namely our security as individuals, members of society, and in a broader sense as guardians of the natural world. This is the reality of the world today and "Powers of the Sixth Sense" is essential reading for every individual seeking to follow a path of integrity within it. Les Munro, International Musician and Martial Artist

CONTENTS

FOREWORD

Powers of the Sixth Sense is an intriguing blend of how our cognitive senses and our psychic or sixth sense can be developed and relied upon for improving our well being and safety, for ourselves and for others. You may think that our cognitive senses are already developed but as Jock Brocas illustrates throughout his book, many people do not give enough attention to the world immediately around them and do not see or hear what is there. Being aware of our surroundings, including information available through our subliminal sensitivities, requires little effort and is a significant step toward enhancing our own safety. When we include our psychic sensitivities as part of our total awareness we can achieve, as Jock has done, a state of being that optimizes our ability to remain safe in a world that can toss many hurdles in our path.

There is much in this book that is timely, practical and integrative. It is timely since incidents of random criminal acts and deadly terrorist activities are increasing worldwide and can involve any one of us. It is practical and packed with useful common sense guidelines on how to actually maximize personal safety in a wide variety of situations in the home, business environment and while traveling. It is integrative and shows us how to be more observant, how to access our psychic sensitivities and presents this in a unified mind-body-spirit perspective. The author demonstrates how the intuitive and the psychic interrelate for both conscious state psychic awareness and psychic access during sleep and dreams.

Readers will be especially interest in Jock's insights on how we can protect ourselves and our children against potential attacks by stalkers or predators. His advice for protection against abuse or even rape should be read by everyone. His vast experience in personally challenging situations has given him front line knowledge of what it requires to survive, including ability to know the mind of the potential assailant or others who intend harm.

Powers of the Sixth Sense not only can help us achieve personal safety but also the safety and survival of our environment and consequently the survival of all living creatures. The author's keen sense of harmony and balance are a central aspect of how to experience unity with others and the environment, and his dedication to perfecting martial arts talents, especially the Ninja and the Budo path traditions, are the route, the way, that worked best for him as he evolved in his understanding of the deeper interconnectivity aspects of the universe. Throughout this book, he weaves incidents, some quite startling and life saving, from his experiences in the British Army and later as an international security specialist and body guard.

He demonstrates what he proclaims, and we are richer for it. So let us learn from him and discover how we can also achieve a state-of-being, a condition of harmony that is actually a gateway for intuitively knowing specific information that permits us to keep a step ahead of those unexpected bolts from out of the blue. As we achieve this level of outer and inner awareness, and can activate our psychic sense, out sixth sense, we become like warriors in mind, body and spirit and can move about, unafraid, amid emerging difficulties to avoid or prevent them. By exploring and developing the potentials within ourselves, we can also maximize the safety for ourselves and for our loved ones and survive in a troubled and tumultuous world.

In summary, the author's extensive experience as an international security consultant and personal body guard for a variety of individuals including celebrities and high risk business executives, are presented here for you to become your own body guard. By doing so you can enrich your life and help make the world a safer place for everyone. The vision that Jock presents to you is not out of reach but is within your grasp, so I recommend that you join him and the many others who have found the way of unity and harmony, the warrior's path, and create a life that is safer and more efficient than previously thought possible.

Dale E. Graff
PSI-SEMINARS-INITIATIVES
www.dalegraff.com

ACKNOWLEDGEMENTS

This book is dedicated to my beautiful wife who believed in me when others did not and who gave me the courage to write this book to help the multitude that read it. Without her constant encouragement and her understanding of me and my life, this work would never have been conceived. She is truly my rock on which I have rebuilt my own temple.

It is also dedicated to my late father 'Alec' who now knows the truth and comes to me more times than he ever did on this earth plane. Our relationship is now stronger than ever.

To those that believe you have everything to gain and to those who do not – you have everything to learn.

INTRODUCTION

Life as a Ninja

Like most children in the late 1970s and early 1980s, I was mesmerized when watching martial arts movies. Afterwards, I would re-enact each scene in my mind and in my bedroom – creating a thirst for knowledge in martial arts. Playing Ninja, I can remember throwing around my parents' valuable historic coins – and losing some of them. To me, they closely resembled Ninja stars (*shuriken*) and I thought they made exceptionally good weapons. I also managed to destroy a vast number of broom handles and convincingly rip my clothes while living out these childhood fantasies.

As a child, I could feel and see things that others could not. I also had an unyielding yearning to learn how to protect myself – in this world and the next. At the age of eight, I began to study the martial arts: judo, karate and other combative forms, but nothing gripped me as much as the legendary Ninja and learning Ninjutsu. At the age of 10, I began my perilous journey. Then, there were few Bujinkan (Divine Warrior School) instructors in Europe and only one in Scotland. I was very lucky, as I was accepted, and so began my life as a student Ninja. Most of my peers were much older than me, at 10 years old I was one of the youngest students in Scotland. The next person above me was in his late teens – the instructor preferred to teach older students.

Spiritual combat

The Ninja warriors of Japan were legends shrouded in mystery. The very name instilled fear and trepidation into the hearts of thousands of Japanese, and the tales of superhuman and unnatural acts of bravery sent a shiver down the spine of those who mentioned ninja. Even to this day, the Ninja is portrayed as an awsome and sometimes sinister assassin with no mercy and no ethics. The reality is completely different; these individuals were men and women of high levels of skill and training who led a spiritual existence, governed by an ancient and moral code in both life and death. They were experts in unarmed combat, weaponry, intelligence and espionage. They understood nature and the rhythms of life, using this understanding to their most suitable advantage.

The basis and growth of all martial arts in Japan arose from the Samurai, the oldest living and one of the most lethal arts in the world, and the Ninja were born from Samurai traditions. The schools are over 1,100 years old, with as many as nine different schools of teaching including bone-breaking, muscle damage and esoteric spiritual refinement. It is whispered among my peers that there are many more schools, though these are held in secret and are only revealed to a few. This is the real mind, body and spirit way of life, governed, overall, by spiritual law. There are many martial arts in the world, but the Bujinkan is one of the oldest with traditions as much as 900 years old and is now a worldwide organization. It is the brainchild of Dr Massaki Hatsumi, the 34th Grand master of Ninjutsu and a winner of many international awards from governments and National Institutions. Toshitsugu Takamatsu (33rd Grandmaster) brought together the Nine traditions of traditional ninjutsu comprising of other traditional budo arts. He charged the young Hatsumi to making the idea of true Budoka available to all true individuals worldwide.

The extract is an essay on the essence of Ninjutsu. Every time I read it, I learn something new from the great Ninja master who passed on his teaching to our master.

The Essence of Ninjutsu [1]

The essence of all martial arts and military strategies is self-protection and the prevention of danger. Ninjutsu epitomizes the fullest concept of self-protection of not only the physical body, but the mind and spirit as well. The way of the ninja is the way of enduring, surviving, and prevailing over all that would destroy one. More than merely delivering strikes and slashes, and deeper in significance than the simple outwitting of an enemy; Ninjutsu is the way of attaining that which we need while making the world a better place. The skill of the ninja is the art of winning.

In the beginning study of any combative martial art, proper motivation is crucial. Without the proper frame of mind, continuous exposure to fighting techniques can lead to ruin instead of self-development. However, this fact is not different from any other beneficial practice in life carried to extremes. Medical science is dedicated to the betterment of health and the relief of suffering. Yet the misuse of drugs and the exultation of the physician's skills can lead people to a state where an individual's health is no longer within his or her personal control. A nutritious well-balanced diet works to keep a person alive, vital, and healthy, but grossly overeating, overdrinking, or taking in too many chemicals is a sure way to poison the body.

Governments are established to oversee the harmonious inter-working of all parts of society, but when the rulers become greedy, hungry for power, or lacking in wisdom, the country is subjected to needless wars, disorder, or civil and economic chaos. A religion, when based on faith developed through experience, a broad and questing mind and an unflagging pursuit of universal under-standing, is of inspiration and comfort to people. Once a religion loses its original focus, however, it becomes a deadly thing with which to deceive, control, and tax the people through manipulating their beliefs and fears. It is the same with the martial arts. The skills of self-protection, which should provide a feeling of inner peace and security for the martial artist, so often develop without a balance in the personality. It leads the lesser martial artist into warped realms of unceasing conflict and competition which eventually consume him.

If an expert in the fighting arts sincerely pursues the essence of Ninjutsu, devoid of the influence of the ego's desires. The student will progressively come to realize the ultimate secret for becoming invincible - the attainment of the 'mind and eyes of the divine.' The combatant who would win must be in harmony with the scheme of totality, and must be guided by an intuitive knowledge of the playing out of fate. In tune with the providence of heaven and the impartial justice of nature, and following a clear and pure heart full of trust in the inevitable. The ninja captures the insight that will guide him successfully into battle when he must conquer and conceal himself protectively from hostility when he must acquiesce. The vast universe, beautiful in its coldly impersonal totality, contains all that we call good and bad, all the answers for all the paradoxes we see around us. By opening his eyes and his mind, the ninja can responsively follow the subtle seasons and reasons of heaven; changing just as change is necessary, adapting always. Therefore, in the end there is no such thing as surprise for the ninja.

Toshitsugu Takamatsu

At school, I was unfortunately one of those quiet, studious types who got picked on and bullied; I never mentioned that I studied martial arts. Then one day, when I witnessed a group of boys harassing a young girl just for their amusement, I became so angry that I had to intervene. They turned on me, but as they tried to hit me, I drew on my Ninjutsu training. This not only gave them a shock, but the effectiveness of my own skills surprised me too. At the time, I was not an instinctive fighter as I am now, but growing up in that neighborhood meant that I had to learn to defend myself. The simple understanding of movement and feeling threats before they happened ended many conflicts before they began. Even then, I was utilizing my psychic ability without knowing it.

At the age of seventeen, I decided to join the army as a combat medical technician. My time in the military proved to be difficult, and I endured some very violent bullying. The reason for being attacked was simply that I was Scottish; it made me acutely aware of how ethnic minorities feel. Nevertheless, I survived the bullying and learned some important life lessons in combat, friendship, and overcoming all forms of suffering including suicide. If I can achieve this, I believe anyone can do it. We are all humans with varied abilities, though in essence we are all spirit, and have the same ability to achieve anything we wish. This lies within the grasp of everyone.

Whilst serving in the army, I was honored to be chosen to help with the protection duties and security of her Majesty the Queen Mother, during her visit to Kent. While my colleagues and I were involved in residence security at a castle in Dover and in Deal, we became friendly with members of the Royalty Protection Squad and my interest grew in personal protection. I trained in personal protection and learned from some of the best in the world. I was now 'on the circuit' (as the bodyguard field is known throughout the world). I made many friends from the Special Forces when I was attached to various units, and their friendship lasted even after service, as we met again during our contracts on the circuit.

I left the army in 1995 and became a personal bodyguard. This meant integrating into a level of society that was unfamiliar to me. Protecting wealthy business executives, their families and their assets was an extremely challenging task that presented me with problems needing quick thinking and a structured response. I learned how to communicate with people from different social levels and ethnic backgrounds, and I got to grips with psychology, learning how to understand the subtle nuances in everyday situations. I trained with the best, from former members of the SAS and foreign forces. Yet, secretly in all my contracts, my intuition was growing and unknown to me; I was using it every day.

I left the close-protection industry to work as an international security consultant for several of the top blue-chip companies in the world. I applied my experience to teach the ambassadors of these organizations how to increase their level of security and protect themselves in hostile situations. I also acted as a security consultant for nightclubs in Scotland and south-east London, where violence was a problem, which gave me insight into yet another side of life and direct experience of the increase in violent crime.

Budo ~ The Way of the Warrior

In my search for true Budo – the Way of the Warrior in mind, body and spirit, I became adept at using my intuitive ability to quell incidents that could have escalated into extreme violence; by pre-empting them or by knowing the possible outcome, I could sometimes change the course of that particular history. In other cases, I became unavoidably embroiled in serious violent incidents that had exploded out of control. On those occasions, my training enabled me to isolate the reasoning behind the violence and deal with it in the most effective manner. I learned that confrontation is nothing more than a form of energy that needs respect and manipulation. My ability to sense the deeper aspects of these instances allowed me to grow in mind, body and spirit, and my reputation in this field became established.

Through my further studies of the art of Budo, the way of war, a discipline and way of life specific to the Japanese warrior – I began to experience deeper spiritual aspects of life, which led to my spiritual awakening.

I have always had an interest in spiritual matters. As a child, I aspired to become a Catholic priest and joined religious study groups. I felt I had a deeper understanding of spiritual matters than most adults did, and I could sense things around me that others were oblivious of. I could hear the voices of spirit in my mind and I could sense energy no matter how dark or light. However, unaware that my sixth sense was taking me further into the realms of understanding life, people and situations, I changed direction to follow a more conventional lifestyle. Normality, as others perceived it, lessened my grip on my spiritual gifts, and I was forced to abandon my truth for what others convinced me was true.

Most martial arts have an element of spiritualism or spiritual life within them, although they use different terminology. Characterized by constant efforts to develop awareness to such a high degree they find that feats of superhuman dimensions seem possible. Many fighters reach a level where they can sense danger from within. This requires deep spiritual and psychic understanding that results in a new perspective on life for the individual. The training is disciplined, yet needs a great deal of patience to grasp its essence. The objective of Ninjutsu is simultane-ously to become one with yourself and with the source of creation, to move with the ebb and flow of the universe – a rare and privileged experience.

An example of this in the Bujinkan is a trial called the Godan test, where a student sits blindfolded, eyes closed or facing away from the teacher. Hatsumi or another suitably qualified individual will then attack and the student must sense the attack from within. Although they do not necessarily think of it this way, the students are developing a spiritual psychic gift. Beyond this achievement, your inner senses will be heightened and it is possible to advance to a plane where spirit can touch your soul (your soul is the sum total of your spiritual essence and is the blueprint of your real self. It is the divine spark of the creator or God force within).

The way of the Ninja is like no other art, and it incorporates the essences of the physical realm, the mental body and the spiritual way. To live as a Ninja is more than understanding movement. It is the under-standing of the universe, its law's, its creative force and coming to the realization that we are at one with spirit, our powers remain inherent in us all. The Ninja is warrior – a spiritual warrior and not as some would think – a fearsome adversary.

How will this book help you

At the time of writing this book, in 2007, I travel worldwide and direct corporations in all aspects of security and survival by integrating mind, body and spirit. I combine teaching the art of Ninjutsu – the art of winning – with work as a professional psychic medium.

Bridging the physical, mental and spiritual is the sixth sense. Everyone has five physical senses: hearing, sight, touch, smell and taste. But there are more senses – inner senses. The most common is generally described as the 'sixth sense', also known as gut instinct, intuition, feelings, vibes, inner knowing or perception. As you develop, you will be able to distinguish between different types of the sixth sense.

Many people already use the inner senses without realising it, but I will direct you in how to use them consciously. You can sharpen your inner sense with use. It's the same as with your ordinary faculties. You can see but not notice. You can not listen carefully, and miss important information. The greater the quality of attention you can bring to a situation, the higher your degree of awareness. Beyond what we normally sense is another realm, a higher mind. To begin to comprehend what we cannot see can change life for the better, and in times of trouble it can provide the vital support we need.

There are no magic answers, but I will show in this book that the level of understanding I have is within the grasp of everyone.

Undercover intelligence

Here's an example of using the sixth sense. Many years ago, I was engaged on a dangerous operation whilst working closely with a police intelligence unit that involved investigating international criminals based in London. The closer I came to this organisation, the higher the risk. In order to gain quality information, you have to be in the main line of fire – that's where the action is. The level of intelligence I was receiving involved me deeply infiltrating their ranks and putting myself at a potentially lethal risk, and the closer I got to them, the higher the possibility of being caught out. They were heavily involved in smuggelling drugs and would kill those who made a stand against them or crossed them – a modern mafiosa. I knew names, dates, places and other modus operandi of the group, including international connections. One day, when I was to meet a contact, things went wrong: the car would not start, my communications started to play up, the phone would not work, my radio receiver kept jumping frequency, and I felt an unusual sense of unease and urgency. I stopped and went into the silence of my own inner world, and in my mind, I had an image of myself tied up, being beaten then shot in the back of the head. It was almost as if I was watching a video in my head, and I could physically feel sensations of pain in my body. The image made me feel sick. I decided to change my route through London and not turn up for the meeting. I felt as if a weight had been lifted from my shoulder. I discovered later, a kidnap attempt had been set up. My inner senses had saved my life. The small signs that had gathered around me all day had built an impetus in an attempt to avert my fate. It worked because I was aware.

Of course, that could have been luck and coincidence. Here's a more dramatic example that's harder to explain away. For a while I worked with Special Branch in the UK, and would pass myself off as a rogue security guard, a military expert gone bad, for hire to the highest bidder. I managed to befriend one of the main operatives in a terrorist organisation that smuggled arms and drugs. I became their fix-it man, passing on bullet proof vests and similar equipment to gain their trust. They came to see me as a man in the know, while I passed intelligence back to my colleagues. One day my contact's brother was killed by a rival gang – hanged from the rafters to make it look like suicide. My contact was distraught, and I encouraged his desire for revenge. He agreed to give me information on a major arms haul this rival gang were planning, so we could set them up. The meeting place was set and I flew in from London. The appointment time came and went, but he didn't show. I spoke on the mobile to my police colleagues in London, who said to come back on the next available flight – no more time or money was to be wasted. But the "no-show" wasn't in character. So I asked myself what had gone wrong and what I should do. When I have a problem, I meditate and go within to find the answer. Find a quiet spot, if you can, still the mind, sink deep, let it roam free and bring what's there up to the surface. Within a few minutes the name of a shopping centre came to my mind, with a picture of a bag of sweets. A voice appeared in my head telling me what to do. I followed it and found myself walking to the centre. As I approached it, my target appeared with children in tow. He said he had been delayed, had run into some problems in his home area and was worried that Special Branch would know of his movements. He decided to bring his children with him as a cover story; on holiday to meet family in Scotland. We stopped for coffee, and looking around nervously he passed over a tiny piece of paper wrapped up in a hankerchief. It had information on the movements of released prisoners who were back in business. I had my intelligence.

That is not coincidence. It is a skill that you can cultivate. It's like an animal using its inner instincts for survival, but it is more than a hyper-acute sense of smell, sniffing danger. It's tuning in to the pattern of events imprinted on the universe all around you. On my arrival back in London, my colleague was waiting at the airport for me, looking rather agitated. He had been expecting me back earlier, I had ignored his calls and he was annoyed. After getting a lecture on a wasted and costly journey, I handed him the intelligence. His jaw dropped. "How did you get that?"

Both these examples point out how situations that might have become problematic were resolved to my benefit, because of my ability to interpret guidance from my inner senses. With the instructions in this book, you can learn to develop and use these same skills.

If you want to know more, and you want to increase the levels of security of your life, there is nothing stopping you. There are no secrets and no magic formulas – you already have all the answers within you. You have heard the saying "Go within". If you want more happiness in your life, if you want more finances, or anything your heart desires – for your highest good – go within.

This book is about using your spiritual and mental awareness as much as your physical strength for your security. It is about integrating them into a way of life, facilitating a higher level of external security. By studying a martial art such as Bujinkan, your inner senses become heightened, and perceiving threats as manifest in thought before the event enables you to take the necessary precautionary measures.

PART 1

1: AWARENESS OF YOUR SURROUNDINGS

I am astounded by the lack of awareness I see in day-to-day work and social environments. Easy targets are everywhere, and these individuals seem very blasé about the information they send out to potential attackers. As you walk down the street, how many people seem to be looking at the street or their feet? They could tell you more about the state of their shoes than what is going on around them. They are targets for pickpockets and potential assaults. Be alert! Avoid obvious risks. Box 1 shows key points to remember in upholding environmental awareness.

Lack of awareness in your environment is dangerous in the physical sense – imagine how much more dangerous it is with no awareness of how to use your thought processes to control your fears and emotions. Your negative or positive thoughts lead to an auric exchange with those around you like a radio and receiver. Others can feed off your fear. So how do we control our thoughts?

Be AWARE:

A – Ask yourself...

W – What was that thought?

A – Accept the thought.

R – Recognize the thought either positive or negative.

E – Eradicate the thought if it does not resonate with your higher self.

We are often told to avoid situations and areas that may potentially lead us into harm's way. However, we never listen to our own minds and our intuition. We are complacent and believe that it will never happen to us. It is amazing to find that so many individuals are unaware of threatening situations or areas that may lead to harm. Use your intuition when out and about, feel your surroundings and develop your awareness to a new level.

Many people tell me that they know of the danger, but they choose to ignore it as it makes life easier for them in the short-term. Could this be a lack of awareness, or is it plain stupidity when we are given the signs to keep us safe from harm, and we choose to ignore them. Be in tune with your surroundings and always be on the lookout for sources of danger. Be especially aware when you are most vulnerable, such as when leaving or entering your home. Don't be lulled into a false sense of security during your regular social activity. It is advisable to avoid creating a regular pattern of behavior. Be aware on entering or leaving your place of work. Wait for a little while before you enter or leave a place and tune into your inner feelings. What are they saying? Are they good or do you have an internal uneasy feeling – react accordingly. Learning to use your natural awareness will allow you to flee at times when danger lurks or take a completely different route.

Short Cuts

Trying to cut a few minutes off your time to make your life easier could get you killed. If you decide to walk through the park at night to reduce the journey time by five minutes, you have chosen to ignore what even your conscious mind will tell you is wrong. Listen to your guidance and take the well-lit route, even if it is longer.

On one course that I was teaching, one of my students told me about a situation that happened in the park near her home. She had left work much later than usual and on her way back home, she stopped at the edge of the park that would have cut 15 minutes off her journey time. She stood at the park gates and looked in. The area was dark and she had walked through the park at this time of night before with no problems – but something did not sit well with her. She went on to tell me the feelings that she had and the events that played on her mind – of being raped. "I saw a person in my mind being dragged behind a bush, screaming, with no help. I decided to walk the long way that night."

This young woman was not particularly spiritual, but she seemed acutely aware of energy that surrounded her most days. She could tell when her workmates were in a bad mood, so she stayed out of their way. That night she did not walk through the park – but another young woman did. The next day the headline in the news was of the rape in the park. My student believes that her own intuition saved her life. Since that revelation, she has actively attempted to develop that ability to help her in her life in every day dealings in work, love and safety.

Opportunist attack

The opportunist attack comes from an attacker seeing an easy target and committing a crime against the target for their own personal gain. Why do you think the opportunist attacker chooses that particular victim? Quite simply, the chosen victim will exude some kind of negative energy, though unknown to himself or herself. It could be fear or they may mimic the attacker's energy, although the attacker will choose a weaker and easier target.

The most common opportunistic crime is theft, from vehicles or from your handbag in a public place. Use your intuition and the advice in this book; remember that security starts with the mind. Imagine yourself in the place of the criminal and the means for protection will be revealed. For instance, if you can identify that leaving a mobile phone in view of someone increases the opportunity of theft, your mind will tell you to conceal it. It is as simple as that. The same principle applies to the activities of pickpockets, car thieves and other criminals. Even if you are minding your own business and begin to feel uneasy in an area, and you see a violent encounter in your mind, you are being warned by your sixth sense – so heed the warning. All it requires is a few minutes to go within and evaluate the images in your minds eye.

Avoid walking into trouble

It is imperative that you avoid entering areas that are known for violence. Within certain neighborhoods there is a mass consciousness of negative energy that forms a constant presence. These areas become known for trouble or violence. Some areas in downtown Los Angeles, South Africa, Manchester and Glasgow, among others, have concentrations of negative energy and are known as places to keep away from. If you enter such areas and sense that your mood is changing from generally happy to feeling irritated, then something could be telling you that you this is a neighborhood to be avoided. Think of when you experience the sensation of your hair on the back of your head standing on end – that's a warning too, especially in a heavily negatively charged area.

If you encountered a group of youths, would you walk through them or change direction or skirt around them? What do you think would be the best thing to do? Remember the old saying that 'prevention is better than cure' – there's your answer.

When environmental awareness is not heeded

One evening, when I was working as head of security for a major nightclub, Brian, the junior manager, came running to the door in an excitable state. He asked me to detain two men in the club until the local police arrived. I asked for an explanation, but he declined to go into detail.

Later, when these two individuals tried to leave our establishment, I asked them to hang back. When they became agitated, I quickly explained that someone had injured himself at the entrance, and we were waiting for one of the staff to come and clean up. It was difficult for them to see round the corner, and this seemed to satisfy them. I could feel their negativity oozing from them and realized that something was about to explode. As time passed, they became increasingly restless, and they obviously realized something was wrong. They rushed me at the door, and I was forced to restrain them in accordance with our company policy. By recognizing the energy that surrounded us, I could prepare myself for what was to come. I held them down in a restraint that prevented any movement. After about 15 minutes, the police arrived and detained both men. Then I learned what had happened and why Brian had not told me. He knew that I would have given him a lecture about raising his awareness and he did not relish that. I was always trying to get him to come and train with us at my dojo. He was also highly embarrassed at allowing himself to get into that situation.

The previous day, Brian had finished work in the early hours of the morning. On his way home, using his usual route, he stopped to get money from a cash machine that was located in a blind spot and not conducive to good security. Brian was mugged at knifepoint by the two men that I arrested the night at the club. As the two assailants stole his money, they held the weapon against his throat and forced him to take them back to his home, where they robbed him of everything valuable.

In one night, Brian had been stalked, assaulted, robbed and kidnapped, and he lost not only his goods but also part of his life – he was never the same again.

Could Brian have prevented this crime? By using appropriate environmental awareness and some very simple, proven procedures, he could have saved himself much heartache and sorrow, not to mention the depression that ensued. He could have planned ahead and drawn out some money during the day. He could have used a cash point in a safer location. If he was trained some form of self-defense it would have given him an edge – his awareness would have been fundamentally higher. When he was standing at the cash machine, he failed to see or sense the perpetrators coming. Perhaps the way he stood at the machine made it difficult to see around him. It's not advisable to stand facing the machine – standing at an angle allows you to see more and notice when things are out of place. If he had studied to learn how his intuitive side works he would have been better able to sense the danger.

Would there have been any windows of opportunity that would have allowed him to escape? I am sure that with the appropriate training he would have been able to stop the crime and been able to save himself. Perhaps he would have felt an uncomfortable feeling and chosen to change where he went or maybe he would have had a sense of urgency to remove himself from the danger prior to the event. My own belief is that there is a window of opportunity in every situation.

Understanding a little about people and how they behave could have saved him a lot of trouble. By shouting he could have attracted the attention of other people to help him. He could have a number in his mobile phone on speed dial for use in emergencies. The staff where he worked could have had a plan in place. I will return to these themes in subsequent chapters.

The chances are that there were signs to alert him of the impending danger. Perhaps there would have been a news article about muggings; perhaps someone may have relayed a story that sent an emotional warning. Developing his intuition would have taught him how to recognize the language of the soul, thus preventing the crime.

Sensing danger

Environmental awareness, physical awareness, and mental awareness. By combining each of these and using your in-built intuition, you can develop the ability to predict events. Students on my courses are often amazed at what they can sense after a little training and experience.

On one training course that I ran for an international oil company, I taught all the elements of awareness and intuition. Through introducing basic meditative principles, I took the students to a heightened form of awareness. After the guided meditation, I helped the students achieve a mind-state in which they were able to sense very subtle changes in their energy field. This sensitivity enabled them to detect the difference in the density of the energy and to feel the presence of other energies. They were now on the first rung of the ladder in developing their sixth sense and being able to use it for their protection.

At the end of the course, I asked for volunteers to take part in a test. This involved taking my new students to a park in Aberdeen, in the middle of the night. It was in total darkness and very eerie. As part of the challenge, I had hidden several of my previous students (including police officers) in areas that were well covered with high bushes and woods – the ideal place for a potential attacker or rapist. The hidden students had been asked to put themselves into the mind-set of attackers, and they were equipped with various weapons. Their orders were to attack any victim they could and to make it as realistic as possible.

When the new students arrived at the park, they were all worried about what was going to happen. I explained to them that men were hidden in the park ready to attack them in a very realistic and violent manner, including throwing them to the ground as if to carry out a rape. If I had told the students what was going to happen before they arrived at the park their minds would have gone into overdrive. They would have started to have doubts and fear would have shown in the aura. By leaving it to the last minute, no time was allowed to allow any negative thoughts to develop. The women became very agitated and some began to cry. When all the anguish and crying subsided, I was able to explain the process in detail and take them back to the mind-set they had achieved when I first introduced them to meditation.

I asked them to go into the park under two different scenarios. On the first mission, I would be with them and ask them to explain the sensations they felt, to ascertain if they could sense danger. On the second mission, they were to be alone, and if they sensed danger, they were to run back to the place of safety.

Of the 12 women on the course, only one person allowed her fear to be fed by the negative emotion that surrounded her and consequently she was 'attacked'. The other 11 women sensed a presence and used their intuition to the full extent of their training. An interesting feature of the failed attacks was the women sensed the attack from distances as far as 15ft from the perpetrator. They had learned this after only a few lessons, and with further development they would be able to sense danger at an even earlier stage. We can deduce that by learning to use our intuition, we are able to step up the level of protection and safety that we can provide ourselves. This is a formidable weapon against the crimes that others would commit against us or our loved ones.

This is some feedback from the women participants on that course:

"On this course I learned to increase my level of awareness in my environment. The importance of sixth sensory training and its use in my day-to-day life increased my confidence and level of awareness physically and mentally. For me, this meant the training could be the difference between saving a life and losing one. When we were in the park at night, I was skeptical about whether the sixth sensory training would have worked, but with the proper teaching I was proven wrong. The sixth sense worked and it means that using my sixth sense can keep me safe in a world that is becoming increasingly violent." *Karen Hardy, Baker Hughes*

"This course has opened my eyes to what we are all capable of. A skeptic by nature, I have seen the sixth sense in action and was amazed at how easy it should be to protect ourselves from all forms of harm." *A Ferguson, Marathon Oil*

The holistic author and teacher Dr William Bloom uses his natural psychic ability in a practical way to prevent him from walking into trouble. I asked him if he had ever sensed danger. He told me about these examples of using your innate psychic ability to keep you safe. "In London, in dangerous areas, I use my sixth sense to know whether to take a short cut down alleys. I also protect my daughter by extending my sixth sense to cover her. I ride a powerful motorbike, a Yamaha FJR 1300," he said. "Before I go out on it and when I am riding, I am careful to stay present to my sixth sense. Over and over again, I slow down and ride cautiously and, sure enough, find a hazard around the corner or up the road – oil slippages or dangerous drivers."

Another example related to travel beyond his day to day routine, when he listened to his intuition even when it cost him money – but possibly saved his life. "We had a holiday booked in Sri Lanka. I felt very uncomfortable about it for a while. I told my wife Sabrina and she said, 'I'm not getting on a plane with you if you feel that way.' I cancelled the holiday and that included losing the deposit of several hundred pounds. The tsunami hit our resort shortly before our intended vacation."

These examples are a perfect embodiment of an individual who uses his natural ability to protect himself and his family. Everyone is able to use this ability and no particular training is necessary – learning to meditate and resonate with universal love will ensure your first steps into a safer place to be.

Be alert. **Stay aware of what surrounds you and what is in front of you, within you, behind you and to the side of you. This will give you an advantage.**

2: YOUR BODYGUARD: THE MIND

During my time as a bodyguard, I experienced attacks on several occasions and in some of the most hostile environments. That I am still here to write this book is evidence that I survived because of the skills I had learned, but also because I was beginning to understand events on a deeper level. I have been shot at, and so have those I protected. I have experienced direct assaults, and my intuition and rapid response have protected me and my clients, my family and others close to me.

It goes without saying that overall fitness helps in self-protection. If you look after your body, and do not let your fitness deteriorate, your chance of survival increases. However, physical fitness is not as important as having a fit mind. Your mind is your best weapon but we are generally too fearful to use it well. If you are strong in mind, body and spirit, then you will feel safer. That feeling is the key to remaining safe. Do not fear, feel safe and safety will surround you.

In this era that is governed by political trends and environmental pressures, we seem to be tied down by all kinds of fears and most of them are not physical in nature:

Will I have enough money or finance?
Will I be attacked?
Will I die?
Will I find love?
Can I live on my own?
Can I really say what I feel?
Can I take that risk?

You may say these worries make you take necessary precautions to protect yourself or your family, but at what price? You become a prisoner of your own fear, and the enjoyment that you should have in your life is restricted by fear of what may happen. You may decide not to go on a holiday or trip, even though you have up-to-date security and state-of-the-art equipment. Fear stops us doing what we really want to do. *Our lives are too fearful.* Fear feeds on our energy, and we attract negativity. If we can understand the fear and welcome the necessary precautions we should take, then we can put up an invisible firewall of protection.

Fight or flight

Fear is not always bad; when a crisis approaches, it shows itself in the surge of adrenalin. Fight or flight? In dangerous situations, we experience a process called 'the adrenalin dump', which makes us fight or run, depending on the individual. As such, fear is a valuable tool. If an animal is attacked, it instinctively knows what to do – its survival depends on it. As human beings, we lose this ability all too easily. We become too comfortable or complacent and often don't see what is right in front of us.

During an attack, several processes happen. It all starts with fear. Fear communicates itself to those around you. It shows in your posture, how you walk and hold yourself, how you approach the world. When you are faced with something you fear, your body responds internally with a faster heart rate and increased breathing rate, and externally with physical signs such as tremors in your hands. We manifest our thoughts so that the fear is shown in body language.

I once had to meet several members of a paramilitary organization. They were visiting Scotland for a large money raising event to support their cause, and I was the lucky or unlucky individual charged with gaining information and identifying other members of the group. The meet was set and I had to travel to a sports hall where their hired musical band was appearing that night. The closer I got to the venue – the more my mind began to initiate the feeling of fear. Walking down the corridor to meet my contact, I could feel my heart pounding. A huge man with tattoos all over him met me at the entrance. His demeanor felt menacing and the energy from him was very negative – further enhancing my fear.

As he escorted me down towards the meeting room, all I could hear was hands pounding on tables rhythmically and then feet stamping to the beat of a drum. It was almost pitch black and I could barely see in front of me. As quick as the banging started – it stopped and lights flashed on the stage lighting the area like fire and brimstone. There before my eyes was the most terrifying sight. A band on stage, that resembled a military unit, with full combat clothing and brandishing AK 47 assault rifles. My fear exploded and I began to exude the energy from every pore of my body. My hands began to sweat and I began to tremble, yet inside of me I knew exactly what was happening. I took a moment, controlled my breath and went within – I began to settle and my fear diminished slowly.

As an unpleasant, strong emotion, fear often causes terror and immobilization. All this is because of thought processes, which scientists see as prompting the manufacture of adrenalin. A negative thought feeds the fear, which then expresses itself physically. Fear can also be felt inside your spiritual body and the negative energy is exuded like radio waves. Other people notice it without realizing and some people can see it psychically. Those waves of fear will be downloaded to another with a similar vibration that feeds on the fear. The aggressor feeds on this energy of fear and this drives him even further. Therefore, the stronger-willed person who appears more powerful will be able to defeat his adversary. To feel power stimulates the attacker.

However, this adrenalin can also be used as a tool to overcome an attempted assault. When the brain senses danger, it triggers adrenalin to aid fight or flight. Adrenalin is a like fuel injection or turbo-drive in a fighter plane – when it ignites, there is no stopping the jet unless the pilot gains control. You are the pilot of your own jet. The trick is to realize at what point the energy begins to feed the fear, and then to re-channel this energy to give you an advantage over any enemy.

Fright

Fear is a kind of language. To understand that language on different levels, you need to be able to interpret it. If a man speaks Spanish, you need to know that language to understand him; the same principle operates in any attack or intelligence scenario. If you can understand what a person or an organization is saying, you will gain an intelligent advantage in business or defense. If an assailant can understand your language, he gains prior knowledge of methods or points at which he can launch his attack. It is a language of the body and of the mind and spirit.

An example of understanding language is when a martial artist teaches you to look into the eyes of your opponent. This supposedly allows you to feel the intent behind his attack. By the time the emotion is manifested as a physical sign, it can already be too late. You must decipher a code that is understood only by your subconscious mind, and therefore you need to interpret a much deeper form of language and communication by learning to attune yourself psychically to the individual's vibration and energy. You learn to read at a deeper level and recognize the intent and fear within the attacker, so your understanding of his energy becomes your weapon.

We fear what we do not understand or cannot comprehend. In essence, fear is an illusion of the mind, representing fear of the unknown and what may lie ahead. It is an element of our own consciousness based on our own insecurities.

Children are susceptible to information either positive or negative. Their imagination creates other realities. Suppose a young child begins to have nightmares after seeing films that are not suitable, and becomes afraid of the dark. While the child is experiencing the fear, the thoughts are created in their mind and they believe they are in danger, so their mind becomes conditioned to fear the dark. As this fear grows, physical signs begin to show. Afraid of the dark, the child cannot sleep well, and becomes over-tired so its health begins to suffer. Occasionally the child is so scared they are afraid to sleep in the bedroom alone. They might believe that something bad will come and take them. Their fear has grown from a simple moment of overhearing a ghost story or seeing a film not suitable for their age.

I would like to describe my own story of how a fear can manifest years later – even after believing that I was healed from the event. When I was bullied in the army, I was given a severe beating while asleep, and on waking I was faced by several masked men. They beat me and assaulted me in many ways. This act of violence upset my sleep patterns for many years after the event. I had a deep-rooted fear of suffering an attack of such magnitude again. I would often find myself reading or studying into the early hours of the morning, surviving on two or three hours of sleep. That was one of the main reasons for working through the night. I had a fear of what the dark may bring. When I could see around me, I felt safer.

I needed to find something to occupy my wakeful hours in the middle of the night and decided to put my experience in martial arts to the test. I took up an offer to become the head of security for a nightclub in the north of Scotland. I finished my shift at five or six in the morning and it was easier to sleep for a few hours in the morning than to spend all night worrying.

Eventually the noise levels of the nightclub became too much for me. My spiritual life was taking over and I was becoming more sensitive. I gave up the security work to concentrate on my life's path with my future wife. Jo helped to heal me from that great trauma, and slowly but surely my sleep patterns began to become normal. My prize was a full night's sleep. Even now, I cannot sleep in complete darkness; I need a little light to shine through – reminding me that in the dark is always light.

One evening, something happened that threw me right back to the bottom of the hill I had climbed. My mother was nursing my grandfather, who was dying. In the house we could feel spirit all around us and going into his room was like entering a waiting room for the deceased. We retired to bed and soon I drifted off into a deep sleep. I awoke to a terrible scream from my mother bursting into our room, crying for help. It was terrifying reminder of the nighttime attack in my past. I awoke with a terrible fear and froze on the spot. My grandfather was on the brink of passing but my mother's upset, anguish and fear had brought him back from that gateway; her screams brought him back from the dead. She also managed to regress my sleeping patterns back to where they had been before. Just like a child afraid of the dark, I had become conditioned to fear it. It only took one small event to throw me right back to the beginning of that ladder. I had allowed the fear to grip me both in conscious and subconscious thought. My wife Jo helped me to understand this and through understanding my fear, I released it. I can now sleep through the night.

Overcoming fear under certain conditions when our minds are pushed into overdrive can be quite debilitating. The energy we exude from our consciousness draws the negative experience like a moth to a flame and attracts individuals, negative entities or organizations that want to harm us.

This outcome is a consequence of the spiritual law of attraction. The spiritual law of attraction is a universal law, what you emit you attract. Like attracts like; If your vibratory field emits a negative frequency, then you will attract others of the same frequency. If you give out a positive frequency, you will attract those of a positive disposition. Learning to control your thoughts and feelings enables you to develop a secure method of protection – it is invisible to the human eye but it acts like an impenetrable wall. Only others of the same vibration can access that firewall.

Overcoming fear is a state of mind

The first lesson to learn is that security is a state of mind. Depending on your personal or corporate circumstances, the condition and the situation of your home location, your office and surrounding environments, you may need extensive security or basic precautions. However, whatever you are likely to face, your personal fears are the main factors you should address. Understand your fears and allow them to manifest as positive energy – your fears cannot harm you unless you allow it to happen. If you feel afraid, even though you have no grounds for fear, you must do what is necessary to feel safe. **Begin by understanding the emotional nature of fear – face it, feel it, then transmute it.**

"It is not wrong to fear, but it is wrong to allow fear to take root in your soul." J Brocas 2005

The most important facet to realize is that you already have the answers. You have the ability to be your own bodyguard, you already know what to do and your attitude to life will change when you see what is unseen.

By breathing slowly intently and rhythmically, you will manage to remain calm in the face of adversity. It is no coincidence that martial artists put great emphasis on the breath. When you are nervous and fearful your breathing becomes tight, irregular and shallow, you cannot think positively and clearly and are feeding negative energy.

If you find yourself in a serious confrontational situation, you might panic as your fears are instantaneously released and your conscious mind begins to feed your fear. Your breathing gets faster, adrenalin is released, and you freeze. When you use breath as the control, you interrupt the feeding of the negative energy in that thought process, and the heart rate slows as you become calmer. You are then able to defend yourself with a true heart and reverse any situation to your advantage.

Everything exists and lives on the breath. The secret to controlling life in a more productive way is through meditation and breath, *prana* or *hara* as it is understood in other cultures. The ancient Samurai, Ninja and Buddhist monks used the breath as the form of gaining enlightenment. In Budo, the Way of the Warrior, the breath exists as the catalyst that strengthens the power and understanding of the universal force that is energy, and you can manipulate this energy through breathing. You can change it from its normal, low vibration to a higher one. This vibration allows the communion between mind and spirit, and allows the physical body to react in a way that is out of the norm, displaying acts of super-normal ability. The development of psychic abilities is within this dimension and it is by this method of breath work that we learn the secrets to the universe.

Walk tall. Keep your head held high, look as if you have a purpose and know where you are and where you are going.

3: PROTECTING YOUR HOME

Firstly and foremost, your home should be a place where you feel safe and relaxed. The energy in the home should be vibrant and have no vibrations of negativity. It is important to maintain positive energy within your home, and to have elements that repel negativity. Positive energy does not resonate with negative energy – positivism acts as a repellent to those that are of a negative disposition.

All too often, people become complacent about the security of their homes. Many people operate on the assumption that 'it'll never happen to me' – but then it does. It is common for doors to be left unlocked, or evidence left around that the owner is not at home, enticing a potential burglar. Even garden layout can be helpful to a thief. Most security precautions are simple. In my training courses, it always surprises me how few people – particularly single women – have even the simplest forms of self-protection such as adequate locks, lights or alarm systems. Depending on the age and circumstances of the victims, robberies can result in people being attacked in their homes. Afterwards, realizing that they could have done much more to protect themselves, victims of break-ins unnecessarily invest vast amounts of money in state-of-the-art equipment. There are many methods that you can use to reduce the risk of crime and improve the security at home.

The following two examples depict typical scenarios of robberies.

Thieves interrupted

Some years ago, after a friend's birthday party, the host's daughter, Debbie, asked if I would take her home. As the taxi pulled up outside her house, we saw that the lights were on in the living room and the bedroom. As she had left the house in darkness, this sight frightened her. We got out of the cab, and I told her to stay back while I went in. As I walked towards her front door, I could hear noises inside that told me someone was still there. I threw the door open and ran inside, just in time to see two men running out through the back of the house and into the garden. I pursued them, but they jumped over the back wall and escaped across the railway tracks.

The living room was in a terrible mess and the bedrooms had also been turned upside down, as the thieves had searched the place. Fortunately, only a small amount of personal belongings had been stolen. The perpetrators could not have been there very long before we arrived. Obviously, this was a frightening experience for Debbie, she felt unable to live there any longer, and she moved out of the area.

However, this serious incident could easily have been prevented. She had no alarm system in the house, and she made no use of lighting in any form. In fact, she made her house an attractive target, and many expensive items could be seen from the windows, there was evidently no one at home, and the back window opened easily from the outside and offered the robbers the perfect escape route.

Security is predominantly a common-sense approach to your environment to recognize the risks. However, we all have an underlying ability to use intuition to complement the physical levels of security to reflect mind, body and spirit. Tuning in to your sixth sense, you can become aware of the potential pitfalls in your security. The response will take the form of feelings or sensations within your body and throughout your external environment of vulnerable areas to protect. In advanced cases, mastering your intuition will allow you to predict possible outcomes of events.

On another occasion, my wife and I ventured out to take some photographs of the highlands. Driving down the highway, we both had the same intuitive feeling that we had left the door open at the house and our laptops that were in the home, were in view from the window. I had a feeling of dread as I could visualize someone entering our home and making off with our valuables. Immediately, I turned our car and drove back to the house only to find that the previous feeling I had about our doors was indeed true. Our intuition, all-be-it on a relatively small scale, had warned us again and potentially averted a possible disaster. These could be the same simple intuitive feeling that you will receive – don't dismiss it, it's there for a reason.

Armed robbery

Many years ago, my father and brother were victims of an armed robbery in our family home. They were treated so violently that my father was put into intensive care, I feel that my brother never fully recovered psychologically, and I also feel that it has had a lasting impact on my mother on a subconscious level. On the evening of the robbery, my mother returned from work and found my father and brother in a bad condition. My father had been attacked with a hammer and my brother had been tied up and threatened at gunpoint. Five local gangsters had robbed my family and made off with all of my father's money. From that day, things around our house changed drastically. My childhood home now resembles Fort Knox. In contrast, that is rather like locking the gate when the horse has bolted.

Investigating how this could have happened, I came to the opinion that my father was not security-conscious either at home or when out socializing. He was a businessman, dealing with anything that made a quick profit and he was a larger-than-life character who was popular with everyone. Nevertheless, his level of discretion was very poor, especially when out drinking, when he liked to impress his friends by recounting stories of anything particularly amusing. There is nothing wrong with that in principle, but it could have contributed to the factors making him an easy target:

- He was well known and discretion was not his strong point.
- He flaunted what he had.
- He was easy to follow and watch, as his movements were very predictable.

- His car had a private number plate.
- He drank a lot, and therefore his self-awareness was invariably low.
- The physical security at home was poor, the house was in a quiet area, and there were various escape routes.

These are some useful tips to avoid presenting yourself as an easy target:

Preserving your anonymity

Unless you are speaking to a trusted individual, avoid giving out information on where you are going and what you are doing. Too much information to others could cause problems. It may seem like nothing more than idle gossip, but indulging in loose chit-chat can be dangerous. Aim to achieve anonymity outside your home and establishments, particularly in and around the areas where you live, shop or recreate. I am sure you have heard the expression that 'loose lips sink ships,' advice given to GI's during World War II.

Do not authorize the publication of your details in telephone directories, the electoral register and other easily accessible records. Keep your telephone number ex-directory. Avoid putting personal information on the internet, as cyber crime is growing and causing consumers millions each year.

Be careful to change your address when you move, as this could cause you more problems. For instance, if your bank card is sent to your old address, unscrupulous individuals may use it to make purchases on the internet. Imagine if one day you decide to buy a new dishwasher and take advantage of an interest free deal, however, as your payment is being processed, you are told that this credit has been refused. Contacting the credit agency to find out why this happened, you discover that several credit cards have been applied for in your name, and there have been purchases from catalogues. Yet you knew nothing about any of these transactions. Nevertheless, your credit rating plummets, and you find that your financial status suffers.

It is also important to protect your refuse bins. In the surveillance industry, information on a target is often obtained through carrying out a 'bin spin'. This means searching through refuse to investigate what useful information its contents can reveal. Perhaps your credit card or bank statements are amongst the rubbish. These statements contain more information about you than you realize. For instance, in addition to your name and address it may reveal your date of birth, phone numbers, account numbers, employer and regular financial transactions. Discarded receipts will give information on what you spend your money on, the frequency of spending, and the places you visit. Fast food wrappers would provide information on your lifestyle.

To avoid this exposure, ensure that your refuse areas are secured and locked. Use cross shredders as often as you can to shred sensitive information.

In more sinister operations, your refuse area and your bin are ideal places to hide an incendiary device or explosive.

Locks and keys

What do keys represent? The fear of human mass consciousness is evident in the key, for we feel we have to protect what we have from outside influences. It is a common problem that most people take their keys for granted, misplace or lose them, and even leave them in ridiculous places. As if no robber would ever guess that, the keys might be on a ledge, under a brick, or most famously under the bin. That reminds me of an amusing story about a friend's wife, who rushed into the pub to give her husband a telling-off for being late home. As she left, she shouted, 'The house keys are under the bin'. Of course, he was horrified, as she had just informed all the local hoodlums how to access their home. That made him leave immediately, to get there before they did!

Good quality locks are essential. Better still, if you can afford to go further, install biometric recognition systems. This might sound like a futuristic vision, but it is readily available. Cheap locks are easier to disable and open, but the major issue is key control.

- Keep a strict check on your house keys, and know where they are at all times. If you don't know, someone else might, and not necessarily, the person you would expect.
- Do not allow duplicate keys to be made without your permission. As you know, it's so easy to duplicate a key, and key-copiers do not check to whom it belongs.
- If a key is lost in suspicious circumstances, report the loss and have a new lock fitted immediately. It's better to be safe than sorry.
- Keys should never carry any form of written identification. Keys with labels identifying them as the front door key are simply inviting theft. Think about fitting a key-code entry system and reduce the need for keys thus reducing the risk further.
- Never leave keys under the mat or in any other obvious hiding places. If I know these hiding places, then you can be sure that potential thieves and attackers also know them.
- Ensure that when you are out socializing or shopping you do not leave your keys lying around. This is an opportunity for them to be copied or stolen, and this can happen very quickly. People who have lost their keys on a night out have been robbed on the very same evening before they returned home.

Doors and windows

Imagine the scenario, you hear a knock at your door and you go to answer it. What if the person at the other side is an attacker or a con man or woman? At this time, you are particularly vulnerable, and if you exude vulnerability, you can be selected as a target. Every year the number of elderly people being attacked or targeted by tricksters seems to rise, even though society is supposed to be more enlightened.

As technology advances so does the ability of fraudsters and tricksters. They are able to produce realistic documentation and fake ID-badges, and they can dupe even the most informed person.

- Do not answer the door automatically in response to a knock or bell. First, find out who is on the other side by looking through an adjacent window, by speaking through an entry-phone, or by using a spy-hole.

- If you become suspicious of any caller, do not open the door. Check and double-check, and listen to your body's internal warning system.

- When going to answer the door, do not illuminate yourself by putting on the hall light. Instead, an external light near the door should be kept burning during the hours of darkness.

- If you have glass panes in the door, prevent observation by, for example, fitting a thick curtain. If you live in a high-risk area, you can fit security film.

- Fit an approved security chain. These can be found in any good DIY store.

- Keep windows locked whenever possible. Make sure that all access windows are fitted with adequate security locks and possibly even alarm sensors.

- After dark, keep curtains or blinds closed. Draw the curtains before you switch on lights, avoiding illuminating yourself and your premises. Switch off lights before drawing back the curtains to avoid being silhouetted at windows. Use lighting-timer devices for your house, office and the outside perimeter. No potential attacker or thief wants to be illuminated.

- Each night before retiring to bed, make a safety check to ensure that all doors and windows are properly closed and locked. Ensure also that you keep keys away from the locks and the access points.

- Get into a routine at night and set it in your subconscious mind, so that it becomes a natural response and you never forget it.

Let's look at this with respect to your intuition. If you utilize your natural intuitive ability, as you approach the door you may feel a distinct feeling in your stomach. Recognizing the type of feeling gives you the information you need to protect yourself. If you feel a negative, sick feeling or if you see a warning image clairvoyantly, that will be enough to warn you of impending danger, whether violent or fraudulent. You may also feel tingling sensations in your head. Heeding your in-built warning system may save your life.

Think of this, if you try to deliberately tune into your higher self, and your intuition every time you hear a knock at the door to identify the person at the other side and the reason for the visit. You will undoubtedly become stronger with your vibes the more you use them, and the more you score a direct hit by correctly identifying the person – the stronger you will become. Now, you do not have to be able to identify the person by name. Just the simple identification of who they are such as a tradesman, police officer or other individual is good enough.

Safety film on house windows

Consider fitting security film to your windows. Although this is simply a plastic adhesive film, an approved specialist should install it. If a criminal cannot smash the glass in your window or conservatory door, he will eventually give up and seek an easier target. It also protects in the event of fire.

Before the recent bomb attacks in the city of London and New York, many of the windows that were damaged had already been fitted with security film. This effectively reduced the number of injuries and deaths. In the event of an explosion, such as a bomb or gas leak, the film would reduce the risk of injury from flying shards of glass. The explosion will crack and fragment the window, but the film holds the glass in place. This has been successfully tested and is in use worldwide in offices and residences. In the Middle East, even windows made of bulletproof glass and safety glass are fitted with safety film. It is an inexpensive way of protecting property. The film is available in different grades, with some capable of withstanding small-arms fire.

Garages, gardens and external areas

Most people use garages and outbuildings to keep valuable items such as sports equipment, tools and motorbikes. This range of equipment would have black-market value, and so the doors and windows of these places should be kept locked. If you allow access to places that should be secure, you are introducing another risk into your awareness. For instance, you are offering places of concealment where a potential attacker can lie in wait.

Sensible precautionary measures are:

* Lock your gates and entrances to driveways on a regular basis. Make it a routine to prevent unauthorized access.
* If you suspect that your doors and windows have been tampered with, do not enter until you have checked for signs of unauthorized access. Call the police immediately.
* Do not handle anything suspicious.

Garden design

It might not occur to you, but the way you design your garden could help you increase your security. On the other hand, the garden could be a hindrance to security.

In an earlier period in Japan, beautiful Japanese gardens designed by the Samurai were intended to be very aesthetically pleasing. However, if you look deeper, you see more. In fact, the design is strategic, oriented to provide information important for battle plans and warrior strategies. Even the choice of flora and fauna would support security around the village.

The gardens would also promote an inner peace and an increase in spiritual awareness – this relates to free-flowing source energy, also known as feng shui. This belief in free-flowing energy to create harmony and tranquility also created a sense of inner security. This approach to design is readily apparent in the cities of Tokyo and Hong Kong. The promotion of inner abundance, peace and spiritual awareness also enhances psychic ability or intuition. Each garden would suggest an individual landscape and rocks within the gardens would indicate a particular mountain range. The samurai gardens would map the area, each specific plant they chose could represent a particular military strategy, for instance; a rose bush with thorns could represent Samurai on horseback with yari (spear). Other garden's may not resonate with battle and as with Shinto tradition would mimic spiritual harmony by depicting beautiful landscapes that promoted free flowing energy and a sense of 'oneness.' Each plant and rock would be carefully chosen to depict harmony – almost like the canvas of an artist.

Compare this approach to gardens you may have seen in stately homes. The perimeters usually have hedges that are dense and high, a feature that precludes the possibility of easy, unauthorized access while also providing cover, so that the grounds and the patrons could not be surveyed. Other plants were chosen for their poisonous or sharp thorns, toxic leaves, or their capacity to create a great deal of noise if disturbed. This hindered or hurt anyone seeking or gaining entry. Closer to the buildings, the selected plants would offer no places to hide whilst waiting to launch an attack. Furthermore, choosing to lay pebbledash or stones of some description ensured that anyone getting close to the residence would be heard, as the sound would carry easily through the silence of the night.

Trees

Although trees may look attractive and serene close to your residence, they can allow an easy platform for anyone seeking access to areas within your building, often providing excellent concealment and camouflage. The ancient Ninja were masters at this form of concealment and used the natural environment as a means to ambush an oncoming enemy. Their understanding of the balance of nature made them formidable opponents, and they used the elements of the earth for their own protection and security. You can also become more secure by applying these principles and putting thought into design. The thought manifests as positive energy and that positive energy manifests into a physical form and is best utilized for your own benefit.

Some people maintain that the more cover and seclusion you have, the better. This is true to an extent, but it is even better to amalgamate all security measures.

No burglar or attacker wants to be seen or illuminated, and his main aim is to get away without being caught. Lighting the area heightens security, as the greater the amount of light, the tougher the target. The more strategically placed lighting, the lower the risk. This is about studying your environment to reduce risk – exercising 'due diligence' with your own environment. Become your own health and safety inspector.

- Your front door should be illuminated during the hours of darkness by an infrared light with photosensitive reaction. This would mean that anyone approaching would be lit up, but in the dusk to dawn hours, the light would go out.
- If you go out at night, prepare for your return before you leave. Switch on outside lights, and use timing switches inside the house. One light should be on permanently, perhaps in the living room, and other lights could be timed to go on intermittently. This will give the illusion that someone is in the house and using the various areas. It might be enough to make the potential intruder think again and choose another target.
- Always have some reserve lighting to hand, such as torches or lamps. This is essential cover in the case of a power failure, whether accidental or deliberate.
- Carry a pocket torch on your key ring. Mag-lights – small torches used by police forces – are also excellent and double up as effective self-protection weapons.
- Garden lights are also a useful security measure, and they can be

fitted on the ground, above ground, or even inside the bushes. While adding to the appeal of the garden, they also act as an effective deterrent. Perimeter lights are doubly effective as they form a first line of defense. If the perimeter is lit up, that alone may deter any potential attack or thief.

- Having your driveway and gates well illuminated are also practical measures. When you drive by an estate or residence with a long driveway, you will notice that the lights are in uniformity along the road. This is not just to allow a good view of the driving conditions, but also to make the residents feel safe and secure, as from the darkness, there is always light. When we see light or have light surrounding – we immediately feel safe. All too often, our minds are focused on what the dark may bring and normally that is conscious fearful thoughts. The Ninja were experts in utilizing light and dark to their advantage.

Communications/Telephone

As a form of communication, the telephone is a great asset; as a form of defense and a weapon, it is invaluable. It has been the downfall of many people, from cheating wives and husbands to international terrorists. Most of our personal and business information is conducted through the medium of the telephone. To intervene and eavesdrop on this form of communication can give others a significant advantage over you. To protect yourself, make sure that your telephone is placed in such a position that, when you make calls, you cannot be observed through windows or doors. Clearly, if you can be seen on the telephone, the viewer knows exactly where you are. The incoming call could be a ruse to get you into the position where you can be monitored, attacked, or simply robbed from other areas of the house.

Is your telephone working? If it is mysteriously out of order, this could mean something sinister. Eavesdropping is big business, and it is easy to plant surveillance devices on your line. This is illegal, of course,

The Highwayman and the Ninja

The highwayman of the past knew how to use the dark and light as cover and as a weapon. When choosing his victim, he was careful not to illuminate himself by remaining under the cover of darkness and wearing dark clothing. This masked marauder utilized the darkness hours to conduct his robberies, and he never struck in an area that was well lit.

In comparison, the ninja (shadow warriors) were experts of the night. The way they dressed and moved utilized nature, and they precisely understood the natural balance between light and dark. They utilized the moon as a formidable weapon. How did they do this? The answer is simple and yet ingenious. They would stand on each other's shoulders, cover themselves with a dark cloak, and use the moonlight to project a gigantic shadow of a hideous shape. 'Shape-shifters' was another name they were given, adding to the spread of confusion and terror.

but it happens regularly. Report any fault immediately and be especially vigilant. Ensure you have the use of a mobile phone and/or pager.

You should be aware of the following simple devices.

Transmitters can be installed in so many places and in different ways, to your telephone line at home or to the main exchange outside of your property. This applies equally to offices and work premises.

In one organization where I worked, the director ordered a surveillance operation on his wife, as he suspected her of cheating. Concealed devices similar to those above monitored her activities on the home telephone, several rooms in the house, and in her car.

Here are a few measures to take for self-protection:

- Keep a list of emergency numbers near the telephone in case you need to call for assistance. Have a mobile phone as back-up, in case your landline is faulty or deliberately damaged.

- When answering your phone, exercise as much discretion as possible. Give no information on where you are or any personal details. The caller's name, address and telephone number should be taken so that you can return the call.
- Telephones fitted with caller display/call return services can identify your number. You can dial certain numbers to block your number from being picked up by the receiver. Otherwise, consider having your telephone number changed and/or blocked from this service.

Human Source Intelligence

This is the ability to acquire information from a target in an inconspicuous manner. Some companies train their staff in this technique, as an unsuspecting individual will unwittingly divulge a great deal of information. The process is to choose a target and identify something that he or she is interested in. This will be used as common ground and can be the key to unlocking someone's mind. First names are used especially to encourage quick familiarity – be aware of this.

The following conversation should give you an idea of how easy it can be to gather intelligence:

CALLER: Hi! Is that Sally?

TARGET: Sure, can I help you?

CALLER: Is that Sally from Albert Street?

TARGET: Sure.

CALLER: Oh great, how you doing? Sorry to call you when the weather's so great. Are you sunbathing?

TARGET: Yes, I love sunbathing. I'm just lying in my garden soaking up the rays.

CALLER: Cool, wish I was too ... though I did at the weekend, got sunburned, and now I can hardly move.

TARGET: Really, how are you?

CALLER: In a lot of pain, but hoping it'll get better soon. Say, can you recommend anything?

What's actually happened here is that the caller has quickly found some common ground and the target is now beginning to empathize. This allows information to be gathered. For instance, he's confirmed that it is definitely Sally, he knows the area she lives in, and also that she has a garden. He's noted that she has a sweet tone and sounds innocent. He could find out even more:

TARGET: Sure, there's a great cream on the market that my friend tried. X Cream!

CALLER: I'll try that, thanks. So you off today, gonna make a nice meal for your boyfriend?

TARGET: Yes, off today but back to work tomorrow. Don't have a boyfriend right now. No point in cooking for one!

CALLER: Cool. What is it you do?

TARGET: I'm a nurse.

Analyzing this dialogue, he now knows her job, and that she is unattached, on holiday today, but not at home tomorrow. This should have opened your eyes to how easy it is to get information from someone just by empathy alone. Be careful what you say. Please note that organizations such as financial institutions will often ask to confirm your details. Confirm nothing unless they tell you what they have first. Use your intuition.

Use your intuition

Ok! So now, you are wondering how we can protect ourselves from Human Source Intelligence using our intuition – you can. When you first answer the phone, always take a little time to tune in – listen to your inner senses. If when you answer and you feel quite apprehensive then your intuition is warning you that it may not be safe. Psychic clairvoyant images may come to you the instant you answer – warning you in some way. I do not know in which form these images will take, but you will know them and only you will be able to recognize them. When I have a warning, I sometimes see a burning building and when I see that – I know that trouble is brewing or there is a problem. Sometimes I will see a firework explode or hear an explosion clairaudiently. On hearing this, I know that trouble or possible disaster is brewing and I can take the requisite precautions.

When an individual calls me to join my Bujinkan classes; I always take a little time to tune into their vibration. Very quickly, I can identify if the individual is the right person to train with me and if their motives are honorable. I take note of the intuitive feelings and clairvoyant images I am receiving as I talk. I then make my decision based on those feelings and to date I have never been wrong. Of course, on the flip side, just the look of an individual can be enough to put you off.

I once held an interview for an individual who was interested in training in my school. He turned up to see me, wearing gothic clothing, black fingernails, scary looking makeup and a top that said "Christ is coming – run." I asked him his name and he said "prince of darkness" My decision was made for me. I told him to go to the boxing class in another town.

Assessing visitors

With the advances in computer technology, it is exceptionally easy to impersonate legitimate visitors such as tradesmen, delivery people and utility engineers, and every year, con men, con women and tricksters target thousands of individuals. After choosing a target, they observe to ascertain if the person may be weak, then they put their plan into action. They normally approach the target and present a fake ID, maybe impersonating a telephone engineer or gas-meter reader. They are often very polite and helpful, and the target may be easily fooled by their convincing act. They might ask to be led around the home tracing wires, looking for points, and so on. The target generally offers some kind of refreshment – in the short time that they are left alone; the con artists will rob the defenseless person of anything valuable they can find.

How easy is it to get a fake ID? Very easy, so easy that it has become a growth industry. Access to the internet is all that is needed. There is a plethora of identity cards available, including international driving licenses, university or college IDs and utility worker identification. If anyone can buy a fake ID, anyone can use them. In the hands of a confidence trickster, it can become a formidable weapon.

There are also more menacing methods that usually leave the target injured and psychologically damaged. In these cases, the perpetrators are usually young and desperate individuals with no morals or understanding of ethical behavior. They are often drug users and petty criminals who will prey on the weak. Preferring a target that is helpless and lives in a quiet area, they may force their way into the property with extreme violence. If there is any resistance, it results in serious injury to the victim. This type of attack can leave people too frightened to continue living in their home, it will destroy their ability to sleep, and it can make them withdraw into themselves. Their lives are ruined, they cannot trust or relax with others, and they become isolated.

These are some simple procedures and tips to protect you from confidence tricksters.

- All visitors should be positively identified before being allowed to enter. This means more than glancing at an ID – instead study it and if necessary telephone to confirm the person's identity and reasons for being there. Do not worry about offending the individual.
- If workers or engineers are calling, then pre-arrange appointments for specific times. If someone calls unexpectedly, do not allow him in. Arrange for him to come back at a more convenient time.

- If you do not know the company, do not allow the person into your home.
- Very late callers should be treated with particular suspicion.

Evaluate the possibility that utilizing your natural psychic ability could save you from potential harm. This is in tandem to your security knowledge you have gained already and the common-sense approach you can take as a normal individual with a heightened awareness of your surroundings.

New babysitters, gardeners, tradesmen and cleaners should be vetted carefully. It is imperative for your own security and your family's safety that you double-check the backgrounds of new staff. It may also be advisable to hire the services of a background-checking agency.

On holiday or business

One of the most worrying times is when you are away from home on business or on holiday. If you plan to leave your residence for a period of days, always check that it is locked and well secured. Arrange for visits to be made by the police, neighbors or friends and family. It is prudent to leave spare keys with a person you trust. He or she should switch on lights or timers; ensure that your alarm is working, and keep your accumulating mail out of sight.

On your return, be cautious. Do not push excessively against a door that normally opens easily, and check around your building and grounds for signs of unauthorized entry. In the event that you become suspicious, notify the police.

As you approach the building, your intuition may sense that something is not quite right. You might see signs around you or perceive images such as an open door. Perhaps you may view a clairvoyant image of a horse bolting from its stable – hence "Too late after the horse has bolted" this could indicate a lack of security. These would be warning signs. Enhancing your awareness will undoubtedly increase your ability to interpret such signs and feelings, so reducing the risk of crime from an inner perspective.

Mail and deliveries

The postal service has been a prime target for thieves, stalkers and terrorists alike. It is an exceptionally useful method of gaining intelligence, launching attacks, planting devices, stalking a victim, and committing acts of fraud. However, the mail is something that is taken for granted. How many times have you received something and opened it without thinking? From experience, I know that mail being delivered to the wrong person can supply a mass of information that is very useful for criminals.

- Do not accept parcels that you have not ordered, or if you have no idea of their origin. Many people even accept deliveries for other people without question. This can be extremely dangerous.
- Do not permit parcels or bags to be left on windowsills or at your door. This lets people know that the property is empty. Depending on the amount and type of deliveries, it can also indicate how long you have been away.
- Deliveries should be checked carefully before accepting them, and the person making the delivery should remain with you until this has been done.
- Depending on the circumstances, it would be prudent to be suspicious of any changes of mail carrier, milkman or other regular deliverymen.
- When going away, stop deliveries of milk, papers.

What can be hidden in the mail? Attacks have been launched on individuals and corporations using easily built devices designed to maim or injure. Examples of contents include razor blades, incendiary packages, explosives, biological or chemical agents, and dangerous animals. The criminal relies upon your innate complacency, and most of the time people do fail to notice important out-of-the-ordinary details.

A shared mailbox is open to everyone that lives in your building or frequents the area, and your personal and business mail can go missing without you ever noticing. Before you know it, you can be refused credit, your identity could be stolen, and your bank account might be emptied – all this from a simple theft of mail.

- You can protect yourself from postal crimes.
- When using a shared postal address, install your own separate box that can be unlocked by you only.
- Ensure that any special mail, such as a new bank card, has an expected time of arrival.
- Utilize post office boxes when necessary. These are relatively inexpensive.
- Do not open mail without first checking its origin.

Use your sixth sense. Some psychics train themselves with doing a reading on the mail. They get the mail in and tune into its vibration without opening the envelope. Later a psychic will open the envelope and find out what percentage he or she got right. Now, if that is a good way to train your intuition – you can be sure that you can use the same training to tune into anything negative that may come to you in the mail. Maybe, we could reduce the risk of surreptitious or explosive devices being sent if we could all learn to tune into those psychic vibrations. Who in their right mind would send something negative in the post knowing that an intuitive would pick up the vibrations and thus detect the device?

Alarms

Consider fitting a 'panic alarm' bell to the outside of the house with switches both upstairs and downstairs. Consider making connections to a neighbor's house or to a local monitoring station. Alarms are a very inexpensive form of protection, and you can buy them from any hardware store. Beware of expensive monitoring contracts, as they often achieve nothing more than alerting a sleeping, low-paid employee in a monitoring station. The best systems are those linked into a CCTV monitoring station.

Alarms can be basic or complex. A basic alarm would comprise contacts on all doors and windows, infrared sensors in all rooms, and panic attack buttons at the front door and in the bedrooms.

More complex systems, priced at over £100,000, range from biometric recognition to retina-scanning access control. It sounds like material for a James Bond film, only available to the most secretive of organizations, but technology of this level is available to the public. One of my clients spent a great deal of money fortifying his home and he was able to access, on camera, any part of his home and the surrounding area from anywhere in the world. He believed that his position warranted this level of security, whatever the financial cost.

Neighborhood Watch Schemes

From being regarded as an excuse for gossip and intrusive curiosity, these schemes have now gained respect as an active deterrent to criminals. Everyone would like to make their house or building so secure that the perpetrator passes by and chooses another target, but it would be more prudent to extend this level of protection to include the local community. The police respect these groups and will appoint a special liaison officer to offer support. If your area does not have such a scheme, consider starting one or get involved in one that is already established nearby. Neighborhood Watch schemes have had some measurable success in reducing crime, but bear in mind that they are essentially passive, relaying information to outside agencies. On its own, this method of risk reduction is not enough to secure effective protection.

Private social functions

When running private social functions, it is important to take into account the level of security required. These forms of gatherings are excellent targets for criminals. Care must be taken in the issue of invitations to large functions, ensuring that invited guests are reliable and present no security risk. It is fundamentally important that the access for guests operates in a way that maximizes security and minimizes hindrance to the family and the staff. Most organizers of events and functions understand this and will work with you on the invitation list to support an event that runs smoothly.

For residences with security gates, the entrance codes must remain a closely guarded secret. On one occasion, I was commissioned to provide security at an event in Oxfordshire, at the home of a household name. It was a private party for more than 1500 people, and it was not a publicized event. The design of the grounds meant that I would have needed an army to protect the place, and the constraints placed on me made it very difficult to provide the level of security that he and his family wanted. During this operation, the personal access numbers were breached; we had gatecrashers and the press trying to gain entry, and we were constantly escorting unwanted visitors from the premises.

Child security measures

You do not need a large bank balance to employ procedures to protect your children. There are everyday simple measures that you can adopt. Remember that children do not see the darkness in others and are therefore very trusting of individuals. They will believe almost anything a person says, and their innocence leads them into a false sense of security.

When your children reach the age when they can understand and retain information, you should begin to teach them about security. Teach from a perspective of fun, but be sure that they understand the message.

- Ensure that children's rooms are not accessible from outside the house.
- Depending on the child's age, you may want to install some form of camera system.
- Babysitters should be acquainted with procedures for opening the door and answering the telephone. Make sure that they can contact you and know where to find emergency contact telephone numbers. It would be prudent to have a mobile phone in the house, in case anything goes wrong with the landline.
- Discourage children from answering the door, especially after dark. I know of an incident where the child was snatched from the front door of his home.
- Do not allow pre-school children to wander from the house or to play in areas where they cannot be supervised.
- Young children should be discouraged from answering the telephone, as they may unintentionally give out information that compromises your safety.
- Do not allow children to collect or open your mail.

If your child is attending school, confirm with the school that they will contact you before releasing the child to the custody of anyone else. If you entrust another person with this task, present him or her to the school personally. In addition, young children should be accompanied to and from bus stops – if they are known to be there at a particular time, children may be abducted from these areas.

- Travel in at least pairs or with a group of friends. This will make children feel more secure. Alone, they become more vulnerable to outside influences that may have a sinister intent. Should anything untoward happen, there is more chance of summoning help when with friends.
- Use well-frequented areas and public places to reduce risk.

- Stay in well-lit areas. Many children will not enter darkened areas, using their intuition.
- Avoid play areas outside the school. This may sound surprising, but statistics indicate that unsupervised play areas are dangerous places. More children have been snatched from play areas than any other place.
- Refuse gifts or approaches from strangers. Children are incredibly trusting and will respond to anything that is disguised as nice.
- Report attempts of an approach immediately to the nearest responsible adult, and tell you as soon as possible. Time is of the essence here. In all attempts to abduct a child, the timescale is a major factor.
- Tell you at all times where they are and whom they are with, and leave contact details. You need to know the whereabouts of your children at all times.
- Never tell anyone what you do, and to tell you if anyone asks for such information.
- Report suspicious incidents to you. If your child is awakened to the possibilities of danger, he or she will learn to distinguish between suspicious incidents and normality.

Child Abduction

We know that child abduction is one of the most heinous of crimes of our age. The fear that we have within us is so strong and yet it takes a recent case like "Natalie Holloway" or "Madelaine McCann" to wake us to the very nature of the evil. No matter how much you teach your children about strangers, talking is never enough. Kids will by very nature respond to a smile, a sweet or a false promise. As I said before, they do not see the evil in people. Allow me to prove this theory. Recently whilst teaching I proved to a family that their child would respond by going away with whomever I sent. I set up the scenario and the parents said that there was no chance their child would fail due to them being exceptionally proactive in their teaching. Guess what? Yes! The kid went with my chosen person and when asked why, the reply was that "he said my mum sent him." It is necessary for children to be taken through realistic scenarios in order that they re-train the subconcios to react in a natural way to a negative situation.

Children are naturally psychic; they only lose that ability due to environmental pressures and following the wish of the parents. It is important to listen to your child for they will be your psychic eyes and ears if you have not been able to develop your intuition. Your child is pure in heart and knows only good – the changing years then pollute a child's mind to the negativeness that surrounds the world. If your child shows fear or backs away from something, then listen to them, don't just shrug it off. Your child may save your life. In conrast, you should teach your child to respond to their own natural psychic vibes.

Using intuition as a screening tool

There are many ways to employ that intuition in every day life. Let's say you need to hire a nanny or a new member of staff – use your intuition as your own screening tool. As you interview, be aware of any problematic areas that could cause a higher risk. Your intuition can save you from making a grave mistake. Just a polite refusal to hire them would suffice.

Time and time again we have relied on methods associated with forms of intelligence gathering – using analytical tools to choose a suitable candidate for a position. We carry out background checks as well as looking at their finacial status to deduce if this person is a threat or will be a good investment. However these tools are not failsafe. Is there another way we can protect ourselves? Yes! We can utilize our intuitive gifts to learn discernment that will help our decision or pre-warn us of possible disasters.

In glasgow for instance, two doctors who recently attempted to blow up the main airport bypassed all security measures and were infact a suppossed pillar of the comunity. Consequently, they were respected amongst their peers and no one would have imagined that they were planning a bombing campaign. It is interesting to note that their planning would have been manifesting strong negative energy and perhaps those around them could have averted this disaster by being aware of their intuitive gifts and picking up on this energy. Is it possible then that utilizing a natural psychic abilty could have averted the disaster? I believe it could.

Even on ebay

One of my other interests in life is photography. I learned the basics through years of surveillance work, and wanted to turn my hand to more creative aspects of photography. I won an award and began to sell photographs to others. I needed to purchase a new more up-to-date professional camera and being a typical Scotsman, I wanted a good deal. I looked on ebay, and found exactly what I wanted and so began to bid. Watching every hour to ensure that I had a good deal and inevitably at the last second I put in another bid and won. It was a tremendous price.

The minute I received my obligatory email from ebay, I began to have feelings of doubt, and my intuition was telling me that this was a mistake. I investigated and everything seemed to be legitimate including the use of Paypal. But every time I went to pay, my inuitive feelings rose more and more and warned me off. We contacted ebay security department and they confirmed that the deal was indeed a criminal ring trying to extort money from innocent people.

The closer I moved towards paying the invoice, the more I felt nauseus and would see clairvoyant images of disasters. I recognized these subtle signs and nuances from spirit. I acted accordingly and averted a negative outcome.

"Trust must come from within, to know oneself is to know the divine power contained within your soul. To understand and know trust is to know the divine and is to be enlightened." J Brocas 2006

4: PROTECTING YOUR BUSINESS

Many of the factors mentioned in a domestic context are equally applicable in the corporate world. In office buildings, the same guidance for locks, keys, doors, windows, external areas and communications. Keys should never carry any form of written identification. If you need to distinguish between keys, use color coding or alphanumeric systems. Keys with labels identifying them as the front door key or safe key are simply inviting theft. Spare keys should be held in a central location not accessible to visitors, by someone who is vetted and in a position of trust. Knowledge of exactly where they are should be restricted to a few individuals.

However, there are additional areas of security concern for businesses, particularly travel and accommodation in destination countries, as well as threats to business specifically from international terrorism. Remember that buildings can absorb psychic impressions be they good or bad, so if a building has a concentrated negative energy, then negativity will be attracted. That can be terrorism or any other criminal activity.

Retaining anonymity

In the corporate context, executives having a drink at the end of the day may discuss their home and working environments, talking about the costs of recent contracts, the hours put in at work, or the money the company has spent recently in other areas. To most people, their conversation will be of little interest, but to the corporate thief, would-be attacker or terrorist, this can deliver good intelligence to be used in planning crimes.

Items that are associated with your company, or whatever you do for a living, should not be left outside your house or in your car where they can be seen. Anyone passing your vehicle could glean information by seeing what you do or the quality of items you are carrying. For instance, if you are a corporate executive, you may still wear your corporate insignia when out shopping or when standing at a cash machine. What does that insignia tell people?

If the company is a household name, it may suggest that you have an above-average salary, encouraging interest in your account balance. Could someone easily watch you, and then snatch the money from your hand? Have they seen you use the keypad and memorized your PIN? They could clone your card from the details obtained through objective surveillance. Maybe they will try to use your details to purchase products online. Someone could follow you home to get more information about you.

It is in your best interest to travel incognito and give no clues regarding your quality of life that may make you a target for reconnaissance. Do not wear items of clothing with a company insignia when traveling to and from work and avoid being collected at home by corporate vehicles.

Try to avoid disclosing your corporate connection to professional and other commercial organizations or utilities. Although they claim to keep your information confidential, they do share it with other organizations and individuals interested in compiling databases. In publications such as *Who's Who* or open registers published by clubs and societies, use forwarding addresses or post office box numbers rather than private or corporate addresses, which may provide information on you without your knowledge – the smallest amount of open intelligence can be enough to replicate your dealings. Internet sites often ask for detailed information, and as this medium is not well policed, there is a high chance you will be conned before you realize what is happening.

You've got mail

Do not locate the mailroom right in the heart of the business premises. This makes companies extremely vulnerable, because many corporations have very little mail scrutiny or security. To prove this point to a company where I was teaching a course, I tested out their system. My course related to improvised explosive devices. Just before I started the course, I sent a parcel through the mail to my contact in the company. It was addressed to him personally and was about the size of a DVD. However, it contained a model of an explosive device. It was sent through the normal postal channels, it reached his desk ... and he opened it personally.

Business travel security

In practice, most companies give little consideration to issues of travel security and focus their attention on simply getting their employees to their destinations. I have conducted training courses in many international corporations, and I am still surprised at their limited travel security policies. Executives have arrived in countries with high rates of crime and terrorism, with no idea who may be collecting them or how they are traveling onward to their final destination. Many of them feel very uneasy in these situations, and many course participants have said that if anything went seriously wrong, no amount of financial recompense would be enough.

Rather than being restricted to themes obviously synonymous with danger, travel security should encompass all areas and all eventualities. Before they leave their home location, executives should receive a travel information pack including:

- Destination country
- Duration of stay
- Travel arrangements, specifying itinerary, modes of transport to and from areas, identification of transport operators, drivers' names, scheduled meetings with local staff
- Requisite travel documentation and visas where applicable
- Local area information, hospitals, police and all relevant contact information
- Full statistical crime report and police department information

- Immediate action procedures in the event of a compromising situation
- Contact numbers
- Weather / flora and fauna
- Medical information regarding diseases and environmental conditions

Before setting off on a journey or keeping an appointment, you should inform your family or colleagues of these details:

- Destination and method of travel (flight details), expected time of arrival and expected time of return
- Person/company to be visited
- Where you will be staying and how you can be contacted.

On arrival at the destination country, never agree to be driven by anyone not already known to you, other than on accredited public transport. Be aware that in some countries even the law enforcement agencies are corrupt. Look for anything suspicious or out of place at the beginning and end of the journey.

Passports

These are the most important items of travel documentation. In addition to being a recognized identity card, they contain a great deal of information about you that would be needed in the event of an incident. Your passport would be an excellent commodity in certain countries, and accordingly it is imperative that you keep it secure. Make a note of the passport number, date and place of issue, take a photocopy, and keep it separately in a safe place. Send a copy to your lawyer, company and to relatives. Check the passport expiry date. If you are in a foreign country when your passport expires, this can cause you endless problems. Write the full details of your next of kin in your passport, especially their emergency contact numbers

Take a second means of photo-identification with you, such as your driving license. Keep your passport in the hotel safe and carry a photocopy with you. If your passport is lost or stolen overseas, contact the nearest British Embassy, High Commission or Consulate immediately for advice.

Transport Security

Ensure that your luggage is kept locked and within view. If you have to leave your luggage in an area that is out of your sight, make sure that the area is monitored in some way. If you have to surrender your luggage, ensure that it is correctly identified; when it is returned to you, check immediately for signs of tampering.

On a train, choose a compartment that is already occupied. Never sit alone or in any unattended area, as you may become a victim of an attack or other crime. Use your intuition and be guided to a safer haven. Your intuition may alert you to individuals that may be traveling with you or in close proximity – remember the uneasy feeling and explore its meaning.

When traveling by sea, ensure that you have a cabin to yourself and confirm that you are the only person with access. Keep the door locked at all times. Monitor the access by placing a very small piece of paper between the door and the surrounding frame. Choose an unobtrusive area, making sure that you are the only person who knows where it is placed. When you return, if you detect that it has been moved, you should not enter, but summon assistance.

Another facet of sea travel that you should be aware of is the places that you will stop at, and the various ports in many countries. Take a moment before the ship docks and meditate for a while. Ask the universe to show you anything you need to be aware of or to guide you to keep you safe. If during this quiet time, you feel uneasy, then you are probably being warned to increase your awareness or not to go ashore. So many incidents happen on cruises that remain unsolved, including murders, abduction and theft. Become your own psychic bodyguard.

Travel by air has changed considerably since September 11th. The aviation industry is now much more focused on the security of the passengers and aircraft. It is increasingly common to be subjected to rigorous security measures prior to traveling on a plane, and you can expect random strip-searches looking not only for drugs but also for evidence of terrorist activity. Be especially vigilant in airports, be aware of your surroundings, and note anything that seems out of place. Do not be afraid to ask questions, especially when you are about to travel abroad. Ask the aircraft staff what measures they have adopted to protect travelers in the light of recent events.

On the way back from America, my wife and I were subjected to a long and arduous security check and singled out because we only had a one-way ticket. The concerns for the welfare of other travelers are now so rigid that they are almost annoying but necessary.

If you must travel by taxi, always make sure that the driver is registered and holds the requisite license. Never share a cab with people you do not know.

Traveling by car

In countries such as South Africa and some areas of the Americas, car jacking is on the increase, and this form of crime has spread to the United Kingdom. The modus operandi of most car-jackers is to catch the driver unaware, often at bottlenecks or traffic signals. Cars are designed with security in mind, and in many countries, anti-hijacking options are available, but the most important thing to remember is to keep your car locked whenever traveling in dangerous areas. Windows should be used in accordance with the 'one-inch principle'. To negate the possibility of forced entry or theft you should lower the windows by no more than one inch. Other measures include having some form of recording equipment installed, like CCTV, and making vehicles bullet-resistant.

Another course of action is to adopt a fluid driving technique. This means driving at a speed conducive to fluid movement with less risk of stoppages, while maintaining accurate surveillance of the environment, reading the road ahead for likely problems or possible slowing-down points.

- Ensure that you have sufficient petrol to avoid stopping at unknown or isolated filling stations.
- Keep the doors locked when you are driving. Open the windows only enough for ventilation.
- Keep to main routes.
- Conform to traffic flow, but keep your distance from the car in front – do not become 'boxed in'. Allow yourself enough room to maneuver, especially at traffic lights. Do not get caught in a standstill at lights, remember the technique of fluid driving.
- Look ahead along a row of vehicles parked in the street for anything suspicious, and through the driving mirror for vehicles following you. Vehicles faced in opposite directions with their wheels turned outwards should be treated with suspicion.
- If something suspicious appears to be happening on the road, stop and change direction or make a diversion. Beware of accident scenes in isolated areas – 'a stopper and a plug' may have staged these. This refers to a vehicle or blockage ahead (which stops you) and then one moves into place at the rear (which plugs the gap).
- Do not give lifts, or open doors to unknown persons.
- When in busy areas, use the one-inch principle when opening windows.
- Avoid using personalized number plates, as they attract attention and are easy to remember.

Safety film on car windows

In car accidents, razor-sharp shards and fragmented glass often penetrate vital organs in the body. In one case, a young man was killed instantly as he traveled down the motorway. As he passed under a bridge that spanned across the carriageway, some youths threw a stone into the windscreen, causing it to shatter immediately, and a sharp piece of glass cut through the driver's jugular vein and carotid artery. This simple case shows how a malicious game resulted in broken glass causing the demise of a healthy man. If the windscreen had been treated with safety film, perhaps he would have survived. Do not assume that this is just for famous celebrities – it could save your life. Your intuition can also play a part in protecting you from possible harm, it could have been in a vivid dream or perhaps you smash something in your home – take heed of warnings.

Security at places of entertainment
Places of entertainment such as wine bars, restaurants and clubs are attractive targets for thieves, muggers and extremists. In general, the security in such establishments is very limited and often inadequate. The staff responsible for security are portrayed as professionals, but if dangerous situations arise they are frequently out of their depth and unable to deal with problems expediently and efficiently.

During an information-gathering phase, an extremist's first port of call is normally the pub or bar, club or recreational facility nearest to the target. In these settings, he would hope to overhear careless talk and build up an intelligence picture by recording the information and subsequently following subjects to their vehicle, residential address or hotel.

Be alert and vigilant for suspicious persons. Report any concerns immediately to the authorities. Do not wear clothing or carry items that identify you with your corporation. If you are out in a group, instigate a shark watch – this means nominating one individual, who should not drink alcohol, to remain on watch inside and outside the establishment and to report any suspicious behavior.

Hotels
If you visit an area frequently, avoid using the same hotel on each visit.

Ensure that the hotels you choose have adequate security measures – do not be afraid to ask to see the hotel's security policy. Most organizations will have a list of quality hotels that they have checked and use frequently. If the hotel has security boxes, confirm that they are manned on a 24-hour basis.

When meeting individuals in your hotel, try to use a purpose-designed meeting area. Do not meet people in your room, especially if you have not met them before. Most hotels have a concierge; they will arrange travel for you or give you advice on the local area and provide an airport shuttle service.

Tune in before a meeting

If you take a little time to tune in or meditate before a meeting, you will amaze yourself at the information you can pick up with your sixth sense. You will pick up psychic impressions of what your person is like before he or she arrives. If you feel uneasy about it, you will know to cancel the meeting.

Be alert to suspicious behavior near your hotel, such as people sitting in cars, tinkering with vehicles, even by uniformed workers. Avoid traveling, working or staying overnight in conditions that isolate you from being able to summon assistance. Always have to hand – or in mind – a ready means of attracting attention.

Let's investigate another scenario – you're a business man or woman and you have just invented a new type of software for the corporate business world. In order to launch this product and realise the vision that you have, you need a suitable partner. Imagine if you will that you are in a board room in tentative discussions with your prospective partners. Maybe all of a sudden you feel sick and there is no apparent reason for this or perhaps you hear that voice in your mind saying *"beware"*. Even after all those warnings you still remain in discussions but before you make a final decision, you experience a vision of a tower collapsing or a building crumbelling to the ground. Would you envisage this as being a message from your intuition? Would you enter into a partnership agreement? or would you listen to your intuition and look elsewhere? Your ability to discern between psychic intuition and conscious thought is fundamentally important. With the right training you will bring yourself to a new level of understanding in which you will begin to notice all the signs from the universe – thus ensuring ultimate safety.

I knew we were bugged

Walking into a business meeting with a client whom I was protecting, I received a psychic image in my mind and objectively, I could see insects all over the place. Rather confused at the image I decided to remain quiet until it happened again. In a blinding flash I realized the room was bugged. When I worked with a business executive, I always carried a handheld electronic countermeasures device. Big business is fraught with corporate spying and I had a reputation amongst executives as being a conscientious operator specializing in protection within this field. I switched on my device and it confirmed my suspicions. I quietly spoke to my client and told him my concerns. My client made his excuses and left. The device was placed under the chair and my intuition had forewarned me of the danger.

He did not heed the warning!

A while ago, an award winning architect in South Wales called me for a reading; he was concerned about various issues that were going on in his life and his work situation. As I tuned in, I could see things that were causing him concern and after he validated the information he relaxed more, and that allowed me to tune into his pure vibration to receive more accurate information. I told him that I could see that 2 colleagues in his office were having an affair and that they were planning to steal corporate intelligence to start their own company. I gave accurate information that could not refute the description of the personnel including the cars they drove. I explained that these individuals were about to steal trade secrets and set up on their own. My client laughed at me and told me that I was off the mark there and I may only be winding him up. A few weeks later in this month of July 2007; the same client called me back in a panic and explained that everything I had told him had come to fruition and that the individuals concerned had indeed had an affair and had stolen company secrets. He asked "what should we do?" but by now it was far too late. Now I am waiting on the call from the company director.

5. PROTECTION AGAINST KIDNAP

AND RANSOM

Kidnapping has now become a frequent occurrence. Corporate executives are kidnapped for ransom money. Kidnapping is now a standard tactic used by terrorists to gain money, media coverage and revenge; and if extremists are involved, the executives are often killed. In South America, there are over 6000 kidnappings a year. Ninety percent of the victims are well treated and in some cases, they even befriend their kidnappers.[2] I know of one employee of a large, well-known US company who has been kidnapped 15 times and is now on first-name terms with his kidnappers. It was just a case of extorting money from the company and he was always the target. Instead of changing any routine, he got Stockholm syndrome and befriended his captors. It then became a game and his company was blind to the escalating problems. Kidnaps of this nature rarely end up in death due to the victim becoming the bargaining tool.

Organized kidnaps rely on careful and meticulous planning, not random opportunity, usually after months of painstaking surveillance. Many kidnappers gather so much intelligence they know to the exact second when an event will take place. They select the easiest target, often someone with predictable patterns of behavior or with inadequate personal security.

Avoid becoming a victim

The most effective way of dealing with these risks is to identify weak points in your personal security and change your patterns of behavior. For example, if you go to the shopping mall every Saturday at the same time, you are displaying habitual patterns of behavior that offer opportunities to terrorists. Adopt simple commonsense security measures. The first and most important measure you can take is to become more self-aware, and this means more than physical awareness. Change your patterns of behavior so that they are not habitual. Become increasingly vigilant and see the unexpected. Take care with the security of information.

Typical kidnapping sequence [3]

- **Surveillance:** Kidnappers carry out surveillance over a long period of time to assess the risks and identify weaknesses in the target's security.
- **Abduction:** The plan moves into operation of the abduction. The kidnappers plan a meticulously timed operation, with several built-in contingency plans.
- **Transfer:** The victim is transferred to a place of holding. This is temporary, as they need to keep moving to camouflage the trail.
- **Demands:** Captors will make their demands after safe contact is established. In South America, this will be for financial gain. In places of higher risk, such as Iraq, financial gain is not the motivation and the chances of bringing the victims back safely are lower.
- **Negotiations:** Trained negotiators are engaged to resolve the situation.
- **Conditions:** Conditions of release are agreed.
- **Release:** The kidnap victims are returned.
- **Freedom:** Before the released victim can go home, a debriefing takes place to gain intelligence on the modus operandi of the organization that carried out the kidnapping.

Survival skills

If you are kidnapped, your mental attitude and agility are the keys to your survival. Maintaining awareness will enable you to absorb useful information. You may notice distinctive smells and sounds, sense direction and recognize your environment, all of which may subsequently help authorities to capture the kidnappers.

However, you could avoid capture if you tune in to the intentions of your captors or heed feelings that warn you off. I have already emphasized the importance of developing your intuition as a form of invisible protection, raising your awareness to a higher degree and heeding it if it warns you of danger. This would be especially useful if you were under threat of kidnap, and it may save your life.

Personal security of children

From my experience working for business executives and foreign royalty I know that their greatest worry is the threat to their children. For kings and queens, the wealthy and the famous, bodyguards have been providing protection for children for thousands of years. The greatest threat of child kidnapping is in South America, where a group known as *La Hermendad* (the brotherhood) extorted millions of dollars from innocent individuals, as a result of collusion between law enforcement officers and a corrupt government administration.[4] In some instances, the children were returned physically unharmed, but mentally scarred for life and in desperate need of counseling. In today's society, there are numerous incidences of child abduction and abuse. There are two types of child abduction: by a parent or a carer, or by a stranger. The UK Foreign and Commonwealth Office recently documented a famous child abduction case, see box opposite.

This example is a relatively straightforward case with a family focus. However, there are more sinister cases involving very real danger, where unscrupulous criminals are prepared to abduct children in pursuit of their objectives of easy financial gain.

The precautionary measures for children at home, outlined in a previous chapter, are equally valid abroad, when children accompany their parents on business trips.

Abduction Case

The Child Abduction Section (CAS) in the FCO received a call from a mother whose two children were missing. She was separated from her husband and the children were living with her. The two children were taken to visit their father for a couple of hours. When they did not return at the end of the afternoon their mother contacted the police and a lawyer, but it was too late, the father had left the country with the children.

For nearly a month the location of the children was unknown, it was believed that they had gone to the Middle East initially, but eventually it was confirmed that they had traveled to Pakistan.

As soon as she realized that they were missing, the mother of the children had obtained UK court orders instructing that the children be returned to her. A UK judge ruled that the case was eligible to be raised under the UK-Pakistan Judicial Protocol.

While details of the UK court orders were passed to the liaison judge in the UK who passed them over to the judge in Pakistan, the children's paternal grandfather traveled out to Pakistan. A case was brought in the Pakistani courts for the return of the children and in the spirit of the agreed protocol, an order was quickly made. The grandfather got in touch with consular staff at the British High Commission and asked for assistance in working with the local Pakistani police to enforce the court order.

Back in the UK the CAS liaised with Interpol and the UK police to see if an international search warrant could be issued. They remained in touch with the mother and passed any news back to her from the British High Commission in Islamabad.

The intense pressure placed on the father on the run from both the Pakistani and UK authorities resulted in him agreeing to return to the UK with the children. The UK police met the father and children off the plane, the father was arrested and charged with child abduction. After seven months apart, to the mother's immense happiness, she was reunited with her children and they have been restored to her care.

PART 2

6: RISK APPRAISAL AND PERSONAL

SELF DEFENSE

What is risk? It is the chance of something going wrong and in that act, injury, damage or loss can occur. To understand risk, you must understand the associated dangers. This statement is a truth of life, and within this truth are lessons to be learned. We take risks everyday and most of the time we remain very blasé to them. A simple act of crossing the highway or taking a trip to the mall is an inevitable risk that we have to take yet it remains simple steps for most.

In the last ten years, blue-chip corporations have adopted the term 'due diligence'. This means they must do everything they can to cover all possible outcomes. This is essentially what we have to do with regard to risk reduction. For instance, let's say you are walking home after work, and the car park owned by your company is in darkness. If the company has not taken security precautions, there is a risk that you could be a target for attack by someone concealed within the darkness. There may be an inadequate supply of security lights, no guards, or the design of the car park may allow a potential attacker to hide effectively. This is an example of one form of risk, but there are many others. A risk can be an element of danger for your physical body: you can calculate the percentage likelihood of the incident occurring and ending in some form of injury or disaster.

Before learning systematic techniques to protect yourself, you must become your own risk adviser. You need to be able to understand risk and negate that which might harm you. Learning to understand your fears will enhance your ability to decode what lies in your mind. Ask yourself:

Is it safe?

- Will I be harmed?
- Will I lose something?
- There are three elements in any attack:
- Target
- Opportunity
- Action (Criminal)

In order to become an effective self-bodyguard, you need to be able to break the chain of events that leads to harm. When you understand the elements of a potential attack, you already have the keys you need. If you remove yourself from the opportunity or from the criminal directly, you enhance your attunement to performing risk analysis. It draws on your intuition. If you listen to your intuition and for the signs from the universe, you will be able to break the cycle and remove yourself from any particular point. By understanding the modus of intention and what intention is – we realize that we can in fact redirect the point at which we break the cycle – removing the opportunity or attack at the point of manifestation.

Mother nature is the bodyguard of life. One must attune to nature and become part of the flow of nature. At this point we become our own life bodyguard.

Understand physical threats
Physical acts of intimidation are perceived through your senses of hearing, seeing, touch and clairsentience. If someone threatens you verbally, it is important to be able to understand the level of threat.

For instance: *"I'm going to kill you"*. How seriously should you take this threat? Do they mean that they are actually going to take your life? Let's Ignore possible medical and mental or psychological issues – put them aside for now. I would say that 95 percent of such threats are unfounded and comprise nothing more than a machismo-style show of power. It is like an animal or insect that shows its colors as a display of strength and a statement that it will leave a bad taste in your mouth if you eat it. This works without a real display of violence, and both parties emerge unscathed.

Unless the individual is psychologically disturbed, these threats have no more meaning than that of the display of the animal using its body language as a defense mechanism. However, the ones to watch out for are those who camouflage their threat, as they are more likely to cause you physical and mental harm. In this instance, you must be attuned to the dangers of your environment and why you are in a position that puts you in danger. Using your intuition and recognizing the negative energy will allow you to weigh up the seriousness of the threat, and help with the decision on how to deal with it.

"Watch your back". This threat can have more impact than a direct threat of assault, as it leaves your mind unsettled. It may cause the psychological state of paranoia to set in, depending on your mental awareness at the time. The thought of having to look over your shoulder constantly is sometimes more than we can bear. From experience, I have had episodes where this form of paranoia has set in.

Use of body language as a threat is manifested in other ways without the use of your voice. For example, an individual who is displaying threats of physical violence may indicate that he will cut your throat by using his hand to imitate a knife cutting your jugular vein. He may point his hand at you mimicking a gun. On the other hand, it could be a simple demonstration of punching a fist into the palm of the other hand to show that you should expect to take a physical beating. People can be threatened in many ways without saying a word. In a court of law, this becomes a difficult element to prove in an assault case, but it still constitutes physical threat.

Protection against a violent attack

For thousands of years, death has been part of the intricate balance of life: in wars, death is imminent, and in violent situations or gatherings, death is a physical part of life. In some attacks the victim is killed. Was this intentional? In many cases, death has resulted from a combination of struggling and violent acts in which an element has gone wrong. However, if an attacker shows his or her face during a sexual assault, there is a greater chance that the victim will be hurt or even killed. This is where you would have to kill or be killed – and worry about the consequences later. It is also important to remember that an attacker may have the intention to kill.

How easy is it to kill a man? The answer is simple: it is as easy as getting dressed, drinking water or eating a meal. A life can be snuffed out just as easily as a flame on a candle. When a person is in the throes of a violent assault, just hitting their head can kill someone, and this has happened by accident. There are numerous meridians and pressure points on the body, and if they suffer trauma from a blow, they can cause parts of the human body to close down, and death will normally follow. You could fall on the ground and hit a vital part of your body that can cause a serious trauma, resulting in death shortly afterwards.

Physical assault is the most obvious form of violence on an individual, you can visualize thedirect cause of the assault on the physical body by cuts, bruises and other injuries. you can visualize the direct cause of the assault on the physical body by cuts, bruises and other injuries. It is the most visible, and it can be lethal. It happens every day, but the signs are often misread and misunderstood. Although victims usually cry out for help, this is sometimes dismissed as attention-seeking behavior. Physical assaults often start small, such as pushing you during an argument or forcefully grabbing your wrist. Perhaps the individual will deliberately push themselves into you as a rouse for an attack. These actions suggest annoyance rather than an initial level of abuse, but this can escalate quickly to grabbing clothing or other items on your body, then a slap, and then maybe a punch.

Physical abuse is any act of violence on the victim, and it can include pushing, grabbing at clothes, pinching, physical restraint, such as pinning you against the wall, slapping on the face, head butting, kicking, beating, choking, pulling hair, punching (on any part of the body), burning, throwing objects, and using them as weapons. Physical abuse can start of as something fairly small and then escalate. Over time, physical abuse usually becomes more severe, and sometimes the severity can lead to the death of the victim.

You will remember that at the beginning of the book, I told you that I took up a job working for a leisure organization. This job tested out my skill in martial arts, intuition and skills of communication. However sometimes it can go so wrong and one small mistake can be a catalyst for a disaster. Where I worked was pretty peaceful and over the time of my authority, I had managed to clean up the place by hearts and minds rather than physical prowess. One night, I knew something was not right, my intuition was warning me of danger and everywhere I went inside the club, I could find nothing wrong. Businessmen and other patrons were enjoying themselves and all seemed quiet. My colleague asked why I was a little off course; I told him that something was not right. Less than ten minutes later, an argument began in the street between a man and a woman. The man slapped the woman and a passing pedestrian got involved. Soon this argument exploded into a large violent fight in the middle of the street and innocent passers by got involved. It took several of my staff, and several police officers to calm the situation and make the relevant arrests.

My intuition was warning me of the impending danger and had I been more in tune, perhaps I could have changed something to reduce the risk of the violent episode. I thought my intuition was warning me of my own area, not one outside my jurisdiction. The small argument resulted in a mass riot in the middle of the street due to the amount of negatively charged energy that surrounded the episode, and many innocent people became injured. One act of violence can produce enough negative energy to fuel a large catastrophe.

Men perpetrate the overwhelming majority of violent attacks, but women are becoming increasingly aggressive, from the Tamil Tigers of Sri Lanka to women that work for criminals all over the world. Men attack with different motivations than women, and their methods are more violent. The weak fall prey to the strong, and this is true in all elements of nature. Perhaps a mistake in the evolution of man is the act of being unaware of our spiritual nature so we remain targets of negative influences that cause violence, wars and abuse.

During the act of physical violence on an individual, the negative energy is pulsating at a tremendous rate and flowing like a white water rapid.

A male will typically attack another male when he wants to fight or if he has a need to show his strength and masculinity, or if he is being influenced by another negative entity. In most cases, men will use some type of excuse such as a violation or criticism of beliefs or physical attributes. Some cases, there is no provocation. The provoker relies on the social and alpha-male behavioral response of the other individual, and the escalation in aggressive behavior results in a violent struggle between the two. This is similar to animals in the jungle, from the lion to the ape. In understanding this form of primitive display of body language, you can learn to turn it to your advantage by realizing what is happening and changing the pattern.

To defuse a conflict, disassociate yourself from the area of concern, apologize, and use any form of calming influence. Hold your hands up in a gesture that is neutral, rather like an alkaline liquid tempering the bite of acid. Do not be cowardly in your response, but speak from a place of understanding and neutrality. Breathe and control your breathing to reduce the amount of adrenalin that is released. This will, in turn control the negative vibrations in your aura. The worst thing to do is to allow the provocation to reach the darkness in you: do not let the negative energy gain in power, remain calm and redirect the energy that he throws out to you.

There may come a point when the situation deteriorates so much that you will have no option other than to defend yourself. If this happens, you must use all that you have learned and strike quickly and effectively, using the provoker's own energy to defeat him. Understand the displacement of energy and know that your true heart will defeat the negative force. Remember that out of the darkness comes light. Understand how your energy flows, and remember in the earlier chapters where I explained how to accept and recognize a negative thought or influence – accept it and re-direct the energy. This transmutes negative energy to the positive.

When a male targets a female, usually to exercise control and power, he does not expect much of a fight from the so-called weaker sex. The aim of the attack is intimidation and humiliation. During the attack, the male relies on the fact that a high percentage of females do not fight back and fear holds them transfixed. In most self-defense scenarios, the teacher normally tells the female not to do anything, regardless of the level of abuse. However, the correct training could save your life. Learning to use your sixth-sensory skills and intelligence will tip the scales in your favor and help you recognize that 'windows of opportunity' exist for escape. Creating the windows yourself by utilizing physical attributes such as your voice will turn an attacker's aggression into fear, as he does not want to be caught – he is relying on your inability to protect yourself.

There are circumstances in which shouting and using your voice can provoke the attacker into becoming angry and venting that anger on you, so you need to utilize your voice and physical skills with precision and timing. Of course, there is another side to utilizing the voice by building your natural KI and interfering with the person's auric field giving you the window of opportunity that you need for evasion. If the attacker is under the influence of drugs, it is likely that the attack will be thwarted only if you debilitate him. There are simple methods of applying these skills. If taught correctly, you will understand that, even in very basic moves, everything should come from a natural posture or stance. The flow is smooth and is like all elements of earth, water, fire, wind and void.

Inside the calm, flowing movement less is more and a very small person can debilitate a large, aggressive attacker in seconds.

I was once challenged to prove this theory during a demonstration I gave at a convention of over 500 women. Engaged to discuss the elements of security and the essence of sixth-sensory living, I was met with the usual skepticism and was told to prove what I was saying. I asked if I could take one woman's young daughter to another area, under total observation from the hosts, and teach her how to take out a 6ft man quickly. The young girl was no more than a child. Then one of my male associates tried to grab her to kidnap her. She floored my friend and left him in quite a bit of pain. *Voila!* On many occasions, I have had to demonstrate the effectiveness of what I teach – it always works.

Attack by an acquaintance
An attack by someone you know as a friend or associate is potentially the most psychologically disturbing. It can escalate from friendly banter to frenzied violent assault, and it does not need to be prompted by use of illegal substances. If a friend deliberately builds up a tension that may explode, he or she usually tests the boundaries by exploiting or upsetting you in ways that seem trivial to anyone else. For instance they could call you names, jeer you about your weight or generally be unkind in response to you. This is tantamount to bullying tactics. As these individuals have remained unchallenged for years, they feel that they have some form of control over you, and when you finally challenge them, it ends up in an explosive situation. The danger in this is when you have had enough and you retaliate. The tension within you is being fed until it reaches a climax and erupts like a volcano.

Rather than get annoyed, the way to deal with these forms of attack is to display some other form of behavior that cannot feed their emotional anger. For instance, if you are taunted and jeered, then rather than responding in vocal form you could laugh or change the direction of the attack by agreeing or by changing the topic of discussion. This confuses the attacker – when you fail to rise to the bait, he or she is faced with an unfamiliar pattern of behavior, and the situation is defused. This form of abuse is detected by your sixth sense: when you learn to open your heart to other dimensions, you will start to feel the negativity in forms of strong pulsating waves of energy. Reading this energy will be like noticing a warning sign and will allow you to change the behavior radically in your favor.

Of course, there may still be a time when you have to protect yourself, and then you must utilize what you have learned physically. I am confident, however, that with the right application of sensory living you can defend yourself with the manipulation of energy and discernment between positive and negative energies.

Defusing aggression utilizing the sixth sense

I was once faced with a very aggressive man who had no obvious grounds for that attitude. My senses told me that there was an underlying fear and depression within him, and that the aggression that he was showing was not his true self. Most people in the business of security with no idea of sixth-sensory living would inevitably fight fire with fire and hope that their strength would prevail. However, remember that 'less is more'. Perceiving that the threat was based on a personal problem, I started to talk to him, establishing common ground. I anticipated that he could strike, so I placed myself in a position from which I could react, but from where I could still talk. Agreeing with him about the problems he might be facing, I was able to allow an element of release into the situation. When his anger had tempered down, was joined by a gentleman from the world of spirit who was giving me the feeling that he was a father figure and that he had recently passed. He confirmed that his father had indeed just passed into the world of spirit, and this man was expressing his fear that he could not face life alone. By just talking and allaying his fears without giving a reading on the street he calmed down, caused no further problems, and went home to sleep it off. I picked up a psychic impression of the real reason for his behavior. When I got home that night, I meditated and my guide told me that all would be well – his father would visit him in dream state to soothe his emotions. I am sure that when he slept that night, he was visited by his father and helped from the other realm. I found common ground with him and by realizing that he was grieving, I was able to be a calming influence.

Self-defense and the Law

The law covers self-defense in any country of the world. However, there are situations when the law cannot protect you, and you may have to make the distinction between obeying the letter of the law and surviving.

The principal aim of self-defense is to reduce the risk of individuals becoming victims of violence by utilizing physical methods that are learned or natural. However, my definition includes giving the term 'self-defense' its widest meaning. I give precedence to those non-physical elements, which utilize all the senses that are designed to ensure the personal safety of the individual. When you learn to use all your senses and become a sixth-sensory person living in a five-sensory world, it follows that physical intervention is always a last resort. You should do everything possible to ensure that you do not become a victim of violence and that you avoid situations that might lead to you having to carry out violent acts. There may be situations where you will be left with no option other than to defend yourself by physical means. You must be prepared for the consequences of using self-defense.

If there was ever any doubt as to the authority for using self-defense, the words of Lord Parker are helpful:

Where a forcible and violent crime is attempted upon the person of another, the party assaulted, or any other person present, is entitled to repel force by force, and, if necessary, to kill the aggressor. [5]

Nowadays, [6]a person may use such force as is reasonable in the circumstances for the purposes of:

- self-defense; or
- defense of another; or
- defense of property; or
- prevention of crime; or
- lawful arrest.

In assessing the reasonableness of the force used, prosecutors should ask:

- Was the use of force justified in the circumstances?
- Was there a need for any force at all?
- Was the force used excessive in the circumstances?

The authority for self-defense is not limited to defending yourself. What do you do if you see a member of your family or another individual being attacked while unable to put up any defense? Would you intervene? It is permissible to use reasonable force to assist another person who is under threat of attack or serious injury.

In a court of law, you and your aggressor will be treated as equals. It would be a different matter, if after restraining the attacker you continued to volley a number of techniques on him or her. If you are trained in self-defense, you do not have to tell the aggressor before you use a technique on him. In real situations, you will not have the time to inform an aggressor what you are going do to and that you are trained in some form of fighting art. If someone targets you they have no early warning system to indicate who is trained and who is not.

It is your right to protect yourself, your family and anyone near you, by the use of force if necessary. It is also reasonable to assume that this right extends to your property and assets. The law recognizes that if a person is under attack or believes that he/she or someone they are close to is about to be attacked, then they have the right to use reasonable force where necessary. To quote Lord Griffith, "If no more force is used than is reasonable to repel the attack, such force is not unlawful and no crime is committed."[7] This is an affirmation of reasonable force.

Reasonable force is another theme that has been disputed. I have quoted Lord Chisholm as stating that, if there is no doubt that your life is in danger, reasonable force can mean killing another individual. If you are about to be killed, or you believe that to be the case, is it reasonable to use a technique that may kill your assailant? I am not a lawyer, and this is a debate that legal observers have been engaged in for years.[8] As an individual trained in some form of defense, you will understand how far you need to go in applying what you have learned. Should my life be endangered in a violent attack, I will do everything in my power to resist, and I'll worry about the consequences later.

In the words of Lord Morris:

If there has been an attack so that the defense is reasonably necessary, it will be recognized that a person defending himself cannot weigh to a nicety the exact measure of his necessary defensive action. If a jury thought that in a moment of unexpected anguish a person attacked had only done what he honestly and instinctively thought was necessary, that would be most potent evidence that only reasonable defensive action had been taken. [9]

Weapons and the Law

Open a newspaper on any day and somewhere in the news there will be details of assaults with deadly weapons. In all parts of the world, this is prevalent from America to Africa and England. Weapons have been used in a vast number of cases, though never in defense; in Scotland, a police officer was attacked with a Samurai sword. It is a disturbing fact that using weapons is now standard practice in everyday incidents. From small-time criminals to organized gangs, the use of knives and guns has become the norm in all areas of the world. The law has tried to banish such weapons, but this has forced the underworld to go deeper and become more secretive in protecting its weapons proliferation program. In every country there are provisions made to restrict access to guns and other weapons of destruction. The truth is that no law will ever stop the basic fundamental necessity to protect oneself and whilst there remains concentrated negativity in the world – weapons are here to stay.

The law in most countries makes provision for times where it may be necessary to use a weapon or instrument to protect you. In America it is everyone's right to bear arms for self-protection – that means guns. If you feel that you are under sufficient threat to warrant an armed response, the law permits you to utilize a weapon to tackle a clear and immediate threat. That does not mean that if you feel under threat you can stick a blade down your sock and carry out acts of retribution. As you would have set out with the intention to use the weapon, it would result in criminal charges against you.

Know the body's weapons

In my study of the Bujinkan art, I have become a great believer in natural body movement or Taijutsu. This teaches that the body is a weapon; in fact, we have an overabundance of natural weapons. The element of natural movement gives you an ability to utilize these weapons in protection of the self. The body's weapons are known in Ninjutsu as the 16 Secret Fists.[10]

Shuki Ken	Elbow
Shitan Ken	Finger End Fist
Kikaku Ken	Demons Horn Fist
Shako Ken	Claw Fist

Fudo Ken	Immovable Fist
Shito Ken	Finger Sword Fist
Kiten Ken	Shuto
Shikan Ken	Finger Ring Fist
Shishen Ken	Secret Spear
Koppo Ken	Bone Method Fist
Happo Ken	8-Leaf Fist
Sokukyaku Ken	Heel Sole Kick (Foot Dance Fist)
Sokugyaku Ken	Foot Reverse Fist
Sokki Ken	Knee strike
Tai Ken	Body Fist
Ki Ken	Spirit Fist

The above collection comprises the body's natural weapons and defenses. The photographs should give you an idea about how to use the various parts of your body to protect yourself in a range of scenarios.

Improvise weapons
If I said to a woman that I could show her how to use a handbag as a set of handcuffs, she would probably laugh. However, in my world 'weapons are an extension of your arm'; in other words, they must become one with

you in mind and body and spirit. When you reach this point of under-standing, you find yourself on a plateau that allows you to utilize your body, mind and improvised weapons in one flowing movement.

These are objects that you could use as weapons: a handbag, pen, wallet, sugar or talcum powder, dirt or stones, a newspaper.

With a little understanding and ingenuity, anything can be used as a weapon, but you need to be taught – for example, what can be done with a wallet? When you understand this principle, it will become an automatic response in times of extreme danger, when your mind will switch to what you have learned. When you first learned to drive, everything was new to you, and it took so much mental, visual and physical co-ordination for everything to work together. You practiced this over a period of time until the process became automatic, and now you engage all senses in a synchronized manner without even being aware of it. This is the state you must achieve to utilize your new knowledge to protect yourself in hostile environments.

Handbag: A handbag can be used as an effective weapon by throwing it around in your immediate area creating a difficult barrier to break through. I teach people how to turn their handbags into handcuffs and trap an assailant within seconds. This takes time and practice, but if I can do it – you can too.

Pen: Pens can be very effective at controlling an assailant or causing an assailant severe pain by stabbing it into the skin or any exposed area.

Sugar or talcum powder: The Ninja used improvised weapons called metsubishi (blinding powder) and as their namesake was used for creating a smoke screen so they could evade capture. Quite simply, these were eggshells filled with talcum powder and fine sand. In the modern world, we can use the same idea. Perhaps you could keep cubes of sugar in your pocket or your handbag. If under attack, you could crush the cube in your hand and throw it into the eyes of your assailant. I often tell women to carry a little talcum powder in a squeezy bottle with two pinpricks in it. The pinpricks are small enough to stop any unnecessary leakage and easy enough to release a smoke screen when squeezed in the direction of a potential attacker.

Newspaper: A newspaper can be a formidable weapon especially when rolled up. Once while working as a bodyguard for a well-known business figure, our businessman was attacked in the middle of the street but unbeknown to the attacker – he had two bodyguards around him. I had used a rolled up newspaper to distract and strike a person with the point.

Challenging mob rule

On one occasion, I was in the town centre where I lived, and several individuals set on a young man. There were at least ten people attacking one, like a pack of hyenas on the hunt. No matter how much of a struggle he put up or tried to fight off, he was slowly being broken down. No one wanted to get involved and soon the negative energy exploded to a terrible violent struggle. Onlookers watched in disgust and failed to come to the aid of the helpless person. I tried to intervene, to help, and suddenly I saw one of the perpetrators stab the shoulder of the innocent individual with a broken bottle. I was becoming more annoyed at the lack of help; I felt a very negative atmosphere and turned just as someone was running at me with an improvised weapon – another sharp implement. I mustered all the energy I could, centered myself and prepared to face the worst and threw as much energy directly at him. I could visualize bolts of lightning coming from my body and hitting him in the chest. The assailant stopped dead in his tracks, looked shocked, turned and ran. It seemed that my energy had affected his intention; another person joined us to help the innocent victim and we stopped the violence just before the police arrived. I am happy to say that the victim survived with only minor wounds.

Recently, when my wife and I were out driving, we began discussing the problems faced by a professional martial artist or any other would be Samaritan, when trying to be a good citizen. Jo described an incident that happened to a friend's husband several years ago, when he intervened to break up a mob that was attacking a youth in her hometown. The mob turned upon him, and he was beaten with a baseball bat, resulting in a long stay in hospital. Evidently, intervention is not always the right thing in such situations. Nevertheless, the laws of karma, right and wrong, yin and yang draw us, and when we see an injustice, our instinct will take over to protect outnumbered individuals. As we were talking, lo and behold, we witnessed an identical scene where a mob was beating another youth. As the fight escalated, the mob began chanting, and some of the youths fell against a car, damaging it. Most vehicles drove past and ignored what was happening, but my wife screamed and insisted that I stop the car and break up the fight. I would not condone anyone to do this, but my experience in many violent situations and my experience in my art gave me an upper hand – not forgetting that I am psychic and sensitive to energy.

I needed to draw on my unique ability to calm situations by exploiting the windows of opportunity. I got out of the car, forced myself into the middle of the mob, and parted the main perpetrators. Please do not try this if you are on your own and are not sure of your ability, this is as dangerous as it gets. Luckily, my size and sheer presence proved advantageous, and I managed to calm things down. As the crowd dispersed and I got into my car, the fight started again, and I had to stop it once more. This time I called the police on an emergency number. At all times, I remained aware of what was around me and ensured that I was in no position to be attacked myself. I had thrown my aura over the situation and sensitized myself to the situation, thus I became acutely aware of all movement. On that occasion, I was lucky, as I ended the incident without being attacked. However, if you find yourself in this situation, survey it first, and call the police from a distance. Do not always try to be a hero.

7: PROTECTION AGAINST ABUSE

Domestic abuse is normally categorized as physical violence on a wife or other members of a family. However, domestic abuse comprises a wide range of physical, sexual, emotional and psychological abuse directed by one person against another. Domestic abuse may also be defined by identifying its function as being domination, control or punishment, within the family unit. Abusers use physical and sexual violence, threats, money, and emotional and psychological techniques to control others and get their way. They will use any method they can to achieve their objective, including using their own children as weapons. Regardless of marital status or gender, abuse can extend into all areas of life and relationships to include religion. In one family alone, I witnessed physical abuse, verbal abuse, sexual abuse and psychological abuse.

It is normal to assume that if one form of abuse exists, a deeper and psychological underlying issue must also be present between the abused and the abuser. In general, individuals that abuse others have experienced abuse in some form or another. They may have suffered from a lack of love or understanding, or they may have experienced abuse through physical violence. As they know no other pattern of behavior, they find it difficult to express themselves in any other way, and consequently, the abused very often becomes the abuser. By examining the reasoning behind the abuse and the stance you can adopt to reduce the risk of it continuing.

Psychological abuse

Threats that are made within a violent relationship can be as debilitating as an act of violence itself. A victim who has already suffered through being hit by an abuser lives under the threat of further retribution. Alternatively, I have known cases where the abuser has not laid a finger on the victim. Instead, the abuser would steal from the victim or try to destroy everything that the victim owned, for example by wrecking the car or the home. Some threats may be part of on-going emotional abuse, and in these cases, the victim is bound by the control of the abuser emotionally, psychologically and physically.

In another tactic, an abuser may threaten to take the children away from the family unit, to kidnap them or to remove all forms of financial support. This is a very strong threat and one that normally gets the full co-operation of the victim. The home environment should be characterized by safety and love, but if forms of abuse threaten to destroy this atmosphere, the victim may agree to anything to keep the family intact. The abuser may feel able to increase the pressure to a greater level, making the victim a prisoner of the family unit and allowing the abuse to continue indefinitely.

A threat of violence is sometimes enough, especially when faced with a stronger and more aggressive adversary. It is sufficient for the victim to hear the threat for the fear to result in uncontrollable emotion. The victim remains in a prison without walls. The fear and suffocating negative energy keeps them locked in an unrelenting circle of abuse.

To overcome this situation, making a stand can be used to deflect the aggressive behavior. There comes a time when you need to take risks. Rather than carrying on as normal, if you can stand strong and call for help, this would be a constructive change – and it may be enough to impact on the abuser's pattern of behavior. Generally, abusers prefer to avoid trouble, and if they sense that they are about to lose out by you leaving and seeking help, they will modify their behavior. An abuser never expects you to take a stand, but when you face the fear and stop feeding the negative emotion, you can become the one who takes control and the individual with the power. Do not feel that you are tied down to the material world, as you have the ability to co-create your own destiny.

By living as a sixth sensory individual, you will be able to sense the beginnings of an abusive relationship. If you can sense this before the event – you will be able to employ methods to transmute negative energy as discussed in previous chapters and thus ensure the doors to the abuse remain closed. You may sense the abuse as a feeling of dred when you are in the company of the abuser. Normally, this will manifest long before the abuse begins and should be taken as an early alarm. When you have sensed the abuse or a have a feeling that some form of abuse may surface – you can instigate the necessary measures to stop it.

Verbal Abuse

Every one of us at some point in life has felt the effects of verbal abuse. This can be very undermining, similar to physical abuse in effect, and it often includes elements of emotional and mental abuse. The abuser usually uses critical, insulting and humiliating remarks that leave the victims hurt to the core of their being. How does abuse affect your energy system? If someone calls you 'fat' or 'skinny', it can be insulting; if your mind suffers from dysmorphic conditions, these insults can cause an emotional imbalance in you. When someone is abusing you verbally, it has a profound effect on your auric field. The vibrancy of the field is diminished and creates weaknesses within the layers of the field. Consequently, the abuse has a deeper effect on the self and can manifest in physical ailments such as headaches, and exacerbation of physiological problems and depression. The negatively charged energy stays within the atmosphere and can be absorbed by another's energy field or even the building. The emotion is charged with that particular feeling and always exists – you cannot destroy it

Here is a useful experiment to try. Stand in front of your partner and hold him or her at arm's length. Get them to stand in a position where their body is balanced or hold out their arm. Now make lovely caring remarks, for example, describing how attractive they look or how you love the clothes, they have chosen to wear. Try pushing the person away or the arm down, and you will find it much harder than if you were hurling abuse at them. Then try the opposite; and hurl terrible remarks of abuse at them by saying that they are ugly and stupid. You will now find it easy to control the person and take them off balance.

In this action, the subtle energy field around you has been disturbed – bombarding it with negative energy has reduced its vibration. When your auric field is down, you are then open to negative spirits influencing you, depression and bad health.

Ever heard of the *mirrors of deflection*? Here's how it works. If you are in a situation where you are being bombarded by negativity then you can deflect the energy using your clairvoyant sight and visualization. Visualize yourself surrounded by mirrors and clairvoyantly see, with intent, the energy deflecting off the mirrors and returned to sender or dissipated to somewhere in the universe to be transmuted into light. Perhaps you could respond with a funny remark or agree with the remarks and send the thought away with a breath of kindness. Another form of verbal abuse would be someone incessantly talking to you when you are trying to sleep.

Verbal abuse can include:

- screaming, shouting, sneering, growling or name-calling
- making threats that include physical violence
- insulting you, perhaps insulting those you love
- insulting your interests and beliefs, and showing no support or understanding
- humiliating you in private or in company, including ignoring you and snubbing you
- withholding approval, appreciation or conversation, never commenting on how well you have done
- refusing to discuss issues that are important to you
- laughing at you and ridiculing how you look or things you do
- leaving threatening messages on your telephone answering machine
- accusing you of being unfaithful in your relationship
- picking on you and annoying you in all possible ways

- blaming you for their failures and making you feel responsible for their inabilities or inappropriate behavior

Each of the above examples prohibits a normal healthy relationship with the individual displaying these patterns of behavior. There is lack of respect and no thoughts for feelings or emotions. In many cases, the person who has been meting out this type of abuse out has experienced it personally himself or herself or is being influenced by an unseen entity. Perhaps this should be a starting point for you, trying to understand this perspective and then to reverse the pattern by showing understanding and love, rather than fighting fire with fire.

Understanding

Mutual respect and understanding are the basis of healthy interaction between individuals, and they promote good relationships, with each individual allowed to maintain his or her values and belief systems.

Here are some ideas to change the pattern:

- Laugh it off. Remember 'laugh and the whole world laughs with you' – such a true statement. Laughter is infectious and it helps to reverse difficult situations. It raises the vibrations in your auric field to a lighter, more receptive level.

- Suggest doing something that occupies the mind. When the mind is busy with an activity that requires brainpower, it becomes increasingly difficult for negative thought-processes to emerge, and this defuses the thoughts that lead to aggressive behavior.

- Find common ground, such as mutual interests. For example, when things appear to be getting out of hand and you feel that the pressure and the energy is building. Change the direction of the energy build-up by switching the mind to common ground where productive, positive thoughts can be released.

- Learn to avoid the attacker's eyes. Divert his focus to another level, and then change the topic of discussion. Attacks usually occur when both sets of eyes are focused on the point of attack.

- Learn how to assert yourself and how express your opinion in a manner that will not excite or anguish the other person. By doing this, you use the 'mirror of deflection', and as you learn each time to be more vocal in your opinion, you place more mirrors in front of you by utilizing clairvoyant images. The negative energy is then directed away from you. Meditate and learn to use the mirrors effectively.

Emotional abuse

Emotional and psychological abuse creates a nucleus for expanding the abuse. Whereas many forms of abuse are obviously cruel, emotional abuse is subtle and quite often unnoticed by victims, they are blinded by their own expectations of life. Emotional abuse leaves psychological scars, not physical ones; it is more mentally damaging and can be likened to a cancer that lies undetected for many years until it is too late. It attacks your very soul and can remove you so far from that which you are and the connection to your divine spark.

There are many categories of emotional and psychological abuse. They encompass a variety of behaviors that will be easy to recognize by those experiencing them, yet often remain completely unnoticed by others. A subtle form of abuse would be financial control, where the abuser ensures that the victim does not have enough money to live or controls every penny. The best way to deal with these types of abuse is a slow process of acceptance and recognizing the good within you. It may be useful to engage in writing down affirmations.

Affirmations

Affirmation comes from the Latin word (affirmare, to assert); it is a statement of truth that when used with intent, is known to re-educate the subconscious mind. It is the realism of autosuggestion, a statement of desirable intention. By meditating on the affirmation, you are raising your vibration to that of the consciousness of the creating forces that will bring the affirmation to fruition. Affirmations are used throughout the world and in many religions; they are used for simple things such as losing weight or bringing into awareness desires like a new job or a new car. An affirmation used for bringing a change within your physical condition, perhaps to stop smoking or drinking, can make dramatic changes in your life. Spiritual affirmations can change your whole out look on life as you become more aware of the trinity of mind, body and spirit.

"I approve of myself and love myself"
This will bring a condition of self-acceptance.

"I am strong, my aura is cleansed and vibrant"
Brings about a change in the energy field through the intent of the individual.

"I am provided for in every way – the universe provides for me in all that I need"
For ensuring that you have abundance in mind, body and spirit.

Control and Isolation
This form of abuse is like the proverbial ball-and-chain caricature or the image of a princess being locked in a high tower. It removes all normality in life, with victims restricted from mingling with friends or family; they become prisoners held by the abuser. In many cases, the abuser regards this as an act of protection and love for the victim, and does not understand the negative impact it has. In reality, it results in hatred towards the abuser and positive relationships can be quickly eroded. This type of abuse can very easily escalate into physical abuse.

Some abusers adopt the tactic of moving home constantly to ensure that the victim is never able to settle or make friends. If the victim does befriend someone, they are normally forbidden to visit. This self-delusion of protecting or worrying about the victim is often revealed as a factor of insecurities within the abusers, such as a fear that they will be abandoned. Isolating someone can include:

- checking up on you
- accusing you of unfaithfulness
- moving to an isolated area
- ensuring you lack transport or a telephone
- making your friends or family feel uncomfortable when visiting, to discourage them from returning
- punishing you for being 10 minutes late home from work by complaining, criticizing, going into bad moods or progressing to physical abuse
- not allowing you to leave the house on your own
- demanding a report on your actions and conversations
- preventing you from working
- disallowing any activity that excludes the abuser
- finding fault with your friends/family
- insisting on taking you to work and collecting you

Anything that singles you out and isolates you can cause you turmoil psychologically and emotionally. Having a strong will and a healthy mind – one that is in tune with spiritual resonance – can help you to deal with the solitude. You will find the ability to remain focused and levelheaded will help you to deal with the problem effectively and increase your survivability. When you are spiritually aware – you are never alone.

When an individual is forced into experiencing isolation, the abuse can fuel negative feelings of anger, emptiness and a feeling of total doom. Isolation can be an extremely dangerous form of abuse.

In the case of an abusive relationship or act, you may have had signs of options to escape the ever-decreasing circle that you find yourself in.

It could be a sign that you see that sparks and element of feeling freedom – you could even hear a song on the radio that sparks your desire to break the chains of bondage. Just a simple thought of making that call to a loved one or a law enforcement agency. This is how the universe responds to your prayers, [11]"ask and you will recieve, knock and the door will be opened" though when we ask and knock we need to be able to recognize the language and the response. Is this why many people remain in abusive relationships? The lack of remaining in line with source, not being able to mimick the flow of energy that is needed very often clouds our judgement especially if we are led to believe that there will be nothing better for us. I believe our creator wants us to live an abundant and happy existance – it is man's incessant greed that causes the misfortunes of others. When we are in line with the universal source, we are able to see the subtle language of the spirit and notice that these signs are the ones that answer our prayers for help. Those who remain in the cycle of abuse and torment are captors of themselves though it could be said that they are also being controlled by external forces. So evil has a name – its name is "the abuser".

8: PROTECTION AGAINST RAPE

Rape is an extremely traumatic experience. It can destroy trust. It can prevent a person from ever settling down again and may prevent the victim from loving again, as emotional scars remain. A rapist can be a total stranger or someone you already know. Even if you recognize the person, you may never have spoken or interacted as individuals. It could be a neighbor, someone at work, someone from the neighborhood; it could be the friend of a friend whom you have met only a few times; or it could be a former partner. Rape is a very serious crime that causes damage on all levels of mind, body and spirit. Rape is about power, control, and anger. Think about the unthinkable. Don't mask the facts with myths and stereotypes. The truth is:

- Rape is an act of violence. It is an attempt to control and degrade using sex as a weapon.
- Rape can happen to anyone – children, students, wives, mothers, working people, grandmothers, the rich and poor, boys and men.
- Rapists can be anyone – classmates, co-workers, a neighbor or delivery person, ugly or attractive, outgoing or shy, even a friend or family member.
- Rapists commit this crime repeatedly, until they are caught.

Just as every crime differs in some way, each rape has a different character. Nevertheless, there are common factors in how the rape comes about and how it is carried out. By learning to recognize windows of opportunity and utilizing your sixth sense, you can significantly reduce and even eliminate the risk of rape.

Rapes by unknown individuals are usually one-off events.[12] When this kind of assault occurs, there is no doubt about the intention. Afterwards, the victim will often ask why she deserved this, blaming herself and often allowing no form of forgiveness. Marital rape can happen repeatedly. Some incidents involve a considerable amount of violence, whereas others are 'force-only' rape that controls the victim and in some cases keeps her a prisoner within herself.

Marital Rape

Even within marriage, if a victim has declined sexual advances, forcing her to comply constitutes rape. This represents total betrayal in the marriage and trust no longer exists. Marital rape is especially destructive because it betrays the fundamental basis of the marital relationship, and if you have taken vows as with most religions – it breaks the fundamental basis of the union. It makes you question every belief you have, related not only to your partner and the marriage but also to yourself. You feel betrayed, humiliated and angry. Your whole life will change, and the effects can be catastrophic. At no time does the rapist consider the effects it could have on people. However, the victim will find it extremely difficult to deal with friends, family and especially the general public. The fear is intensified and the cycle continues.

Rape by someone unknown to you is an act of sexual violence. However, marital rape is not categorized here as a deliberate act of violence, but as an act within an abusive relationship. Such circumstances must be treated as abusive relationships with physical, mental, emotional and spiritual impacts. This often represents long-term abuse and can escalate into a very serious condition. Often, the abused can commit desperate acts to free themselves including murdering the abuser.

One of the differences between rape by someone who is not known to you (referred to as alien rape) and an intimate rape is that alien rape frequently involves a degree of physical violence. This is of course unless an illegal substance such as the well-known date rape drug has been used. In comparison, in marital rape the partner can be coerced into allowing the sexual act to take place. There must be many women who feel that they have been raped. Nevertheless, they seem powerless. In some cases, the husband may believe he is doing nothing wrong as it is within the marriage. Psychologically the victim may display signs of guilt, feeling that somehow it is her fault and that she has caused these problems to occur. The rapist is damaging her on all levels of mind, body and spirit.

Women who experience marital rape have great difficulty in defining it as such due to relationship between the husband and the wife. In the traditional belief system, it is assumed that the marriage vows entitle a man to have sexual relations with his wife at any time of day or night, and this approach is still prevalent in our society. A further issue is that if a husband rapes his wife, she will look for reasons to deny that it really was rape. This is partly because of the psychological hurdle she must overcome in accepting that she had been raped, but also because of loyalty, meaning that she would not want to get her husband into serious trouble.

Remember that if you say no and the act continues, then it is rape. We cannot avoid the truth that rape has been with us for thousands of years, but many women are beginning to challenge this assumption, moving beyond the traditional rules of behavior. The age of women in power has arrived, and they are saying no on more than one level. I hope that we are all learning to treat everyone as equals.

Violent rape involves extreme physical violence. Many abusers will force the victims to submit to sexual acts to which they would never normally consent. In a marital relationship, the victim might understand this compliance as a gesture of forgiveness – and so the cycle of rape continues.

Forceful rape entails using enough force to control the victim, either to hold her in position or to make her do as asked. This is usually the pattern where the abuser has greater physical size and strength. On some occasions, forceful rape may involve a level of emotional abuse and even financial abuse. The victim is locked into a guilt complex that she must satisfy the rapist.

There have been cases where young females have been kidnapped, and then forced to commit sadistic sexual acts for the entertainment of a group of rapists. This type of rape very often includes violence and other characteristics of various types of rape.

Many victims develop a guilt complex about their inability to protect themselves and the fact that they did not try to escape, even though an attempt to escape could have caused more problems.

There are numerous reasons why a woman may be reluctant to fight off a rapist. For example, she will be shocked and confused and these events might cause temporary paralysis; or she may not want to alarm her children or other individuals sleeping nearby, or risk that they would witness the rape. In cases where there is a special bond between the victim and the rapist she may be concerned for the abuser, and unwilling to do anything that might harm or injure him.

Research findings indicate that in an abusive relationship, the woman is most likely to be subjected to rape towards the end of the relationship.[13] Even after she has left, it is highly likely that the abuse will continue in some form when other control tactics, such as isolation or emotional abuse, are no longer effective. This can also prompt the abuser to turn to rape, representing psychological punishment for leaving him. This emotional blackmail can be powerful enough to force the weaker-willed person back into the arms of the abuser.

Understanding the mind of a rapist

A number of men convicted of rape (including date rape) were questioned on how they choose potential victims. [14]

Hairstyle was the first thing on their list. They are most likely to go after a woman with a ponytail, bun, braid or long hair – essentially any hairstyle that can be gripped easily. Women with short hair are not common targets. The second factor they consider is clothing. They prefer women whose clothing is easy to remove quickly. In case of difficulty, many of them carry scissors to cut clothing. They also look for women who are talking on mobile phones, searching through their purse, or distracted by other activities while walking. This means they are off guard and can be more easily overpowered.

The time of day most favored for attack and rape is the early morning, between five and 8.30 am. The number one place where women are attacked or abducted is grocery store parking lots. Number two is office parking lots or garages. Number three is public toilets. These men are looking to grab a woman and quickly move her to a second location where they do not have to worry about being caught.

If you put up any kind of a fight, they get discouraged because it takes only a few minutes for them to realize that struggling with you is not worth it because it will be time-consuming. These men said they would not pick on women who are carrying umbrellas or similar objects that can be used from a distance. Keys are not a deterrent because you have to be really close to the attacker to use them as a weapon. Therefore, your best option is to convince the people you are not worth the trouble. There are several defense mechanisms you could use.

Protect yourself

Use your head and be alert! Walk with confidence and purpose. Utilize your intuitive ability and try to sense the danger before it happens. Remember the discussion on awareness, and how the ability to sense your immediate surroundings can keep you alive? Be careful when out drinking and always keep your drink close to you and in sight: this is the first preventative measure in reducing the risk of you being drugged. If your instinct tells you that it is unsafe, then listen to it.

Inside your home

Ensure that all doors (including sliding glass doors) and windows have sturdy, well-installed locks, and use them. Fit a wide-angle spy hole in the main door and keep entrances well lit. You may decide to install panic alarms within easy reach.

Never open your door to strangers. Check the identification of any sales representatives or service personnel before letting them in. Do not be embarrassed to phone their company for verification. Use your intuition.

If you are asked to make an emergency call, ask the individual to wait outside.

Know your neighbors, so you have someone to call or go to if you are scared. If you arrive home and see a door or window open, or broken, do not go in. Call the police from a mobile phone, a public booth or a neighbor's home.

Do not enter isolated areas on your own. This includes empty apartments, laundry rooms, underground garages, parking areas, and offices after business hours. Walk with a friend, co-worker, or security guard, particularly at night.

Outdoors

Avoid walking or jogging alone, especially at night. Stay in well-lit areas, where there are people around. If you think you're being followed, change direction and head for open stores, restaurants, theatres, or a house.

Wear clothes and shoes that give you freedom of movement. Be cautious if anyone in a car asks you for directions. If you answer, keep your distance from the car, and ensure that you have something in your hands that you could use to strike them. Carry a personal alarm or improvised weapon. If you are ever assaulted, you will be glad you were carrying it or had it concealed in your car.

Before you get in to your car, look around it and check the back seat. Always lock your car – when you get in and when you get out. Try to park in areas that will be well lit and areas that are busy on your return.

Have your key ready before you reach the door – this relates equally to home, office or car doors. So many unprepared women spend time searching their handbags for their keys, hindered by the range of items in the bag. If it takes a very long time, it significantly increases the risk of an opportunistic attack.

What's in the back seat?

This is not meant to frighten you, but be assured that the following actually happened and the young woman was very lucky not to be attacked. A young woman stopped to fill her car up with fuel as she has done hundreds of times. After she filled the tank, she went into the shop to pay for her fuel. Meanwhile, a youth had noticed that she had left her vehicle unattended and hid in the car. Only when a man shouted out at having seen this concealment did the potential attacker get out and run off. It took the young woman a number of weeks to get over this situation and face the reality that she could have been attacked and raped. It just goes to show how easy it can be.

It is imperative that you lock your vehicle every time you leave it unattended. This will not only protect your valuables but protect you as well. So many individuals walk away, never realizing that they have left their vehicles unattended and open to opportunistic crimes. This opportunity might be used to rob you or perhaps even attack you.

If your car breaks down, lift the hood, lock the doors, and turn on your hazard lights. If someone stops, roll the window down slightly to talk. If you have not already phoned for roadside assistance, ask this person to call the police or a recovery service.

Never hitchhike, and never pick up hitchhikers. Attacks and rapes involving hitchhikers and drivers are more numerous than any other motoring incident. Some years ago, the risks may have been minimal, but nowadays you should not trust anyone you do not know – you may be putting your life in their hands. Use your instinct to stay alive.

Dealing with an attack

How should you handle an attempted rape? It depends on a number of factors, such as the location, the rapist's determination, and your physical and emotional state. Surviving is the goal. There is a plethora of techniques to protect you and prevent rape. Of course, it is best to use your intuition and never to put yourself in the line of fire. Nevertheless, if you need to protect yourself, you must do so with conviction.

- If you are being followed along the street or in a garage, or perhaps into an elevator or stairwell, look him in the face and ask a question, such as what time is it? or make small talk, about the weather. Now you have seen his face and you could identify him in a line-up, so you lose your appeal as a target.
- Remember that you are looking for windows of opportunity and these will always present themselves. Try to remain calm and stay in a positive mindset. Talk with him, stall for as long as you can while you assess your options.
- If you are attacked with obvious intent to rape, make as much noise as you can – shouting and screaming. This will discourage your attacker and reduce the chances of him following you. The more noise you make, the more you upset his balance without physical attachment.
- If someone is coming toward you with obvious intent, hold your hands out in front of you and yell 'Stop' or 'Stay back!' If you shout or show that you would not be afraid to fight back, there is a greater chance you will be left alone. Remember that these Individuals are looking for an easy target. If you carry pepper spray, shouting 'I have pepper spray!' and holding it out will be a deterrent. Use your keys or a rolled up newspaper, or better still, talcum powder.
- If a man puts his hands up to you, grab his first two fingers and bend them back as far as possible, pushing them down with as much pressure as you can manage. If you can, strike him quickly in the throat and escape.
- If he grabs hold of you, it is unlikely you will beat him with strength, but you can still outsmart him. If you are grabbed around the waist from behind, pinch the attacker either under the arm between the elbow and armpit or in the upper inner thigh – hard.

Try pinching yourself in those places as hard as you can stand it – it hurts. One woman who used this technique during an attempted date rape broke through the skin and tore out muscle strands – the abuser needed stitches. After the initial hit, always go for the groin. If you hit a man there, it is extremely painful.

- At some point, the rapist will have to relax some part of his body to make the next move – this is when you strike. Utilize the elements of nature and disturb the balance of events. These are your windows and you direct your attack at the weakest point.
- Do whatever it takes to survive. If you decide to fight back, you must be quick, determined and effective. Target the eyes – if a rapist cannot see, you have the advantage.

If the rapist has a weapon, you may have no choice but to submit. However, the weapon will generally be there to scare you, not to harm you. You might think that these actions would anger your attacker and make him want to hurt you more. However, rapists want a woman who will not cause a lot of trouble. If you start causing trouble, he will soon be gone.

Always be aware of your surroundings, take someone with you if you can and if you see any odd behavior, don't dismiss it, just go with your instincts. You may feel silly at the time, but you would feel much worse if the person really was trouble.

Surviving rape

If you are the victim of rape:

- Report it to the police or rape crisis centre. The sooner you report it, the greater the chances that the rapist will be caught.
- Preserve all physical evidence. Do not shower, bathe, change clothes, douche, or throw any clothing away until the police or rape counselor says it is okay.

- Go to a hospital emergency room or your own doctor for medical care immediately.
- Don't go alone. Ask a friend or family member to go with you or call a rape crisis centre or school counselor.
- Remember that rape is not your fault. Do not accept blame for being an innocent victim.
- Get counseling to help deal with feelings of anger, helplessness, fear, and shame caused by rape It helps to talk to someone about the rape, whether it happened last night, last week, or years ago.

If someone you know has been raped:

- Believe her or him.
- Don't blame the victim.
- Offer support, patience and compassion to help the rape victim work through the crisis, heal, and emerge as a survivor.

Promote rape awareness

Try to find a workshop in your area about the risks of rape. Neighborhood watch groups, schools, employers, churches, libraries, police or civic groups, usually hold these regularly. If you cannot find one, you might consider starting a workshop on preventing rape. Make sure it addresses concerns of both men and women. Ask an expert in rape assessment and prevention techniques to show you the reality of how you can protect yourself. You could also volunteer to help at a rape crisis centre; these venues always need help, as there are more rapes than statistics suggest.

If you see a television program or film that reinforces sexual stereotypes and sends the message that women really like to be raped, complain about it. Write to the station, the studio, or the sponsors. On the other hand, if the media do a good job of depicting the realities of rape, publicly praise them for it.

If you start a rape-awareness group, you will receive support from organizations and law enforcement agencies to promote it. If you invite a martial artist to address the group, choose one who goes beyond techniques and who clearly understands mind, body and spirit. As a sixth-sensory individual, you can enhance all levels of prevention.

9: TERRORISM

The very mention of terrorism strikes fear into the hearts of most individuals. It conjures up images of violence or the threat of violence, especially bombing, kidnapping and assassination, usually carried out for political purposes. The Oxford Dictionary of English defines it as 'the unofficial or unauthorized use of violence and intimidation in the pursuit of political aims'.

The aims and objectives of terrorists are to gain public support or credibility, usually within their own country. They are driven by religious objectives and the wish to assume political power. Nevertheless, it has been observed that 'one man's terrorist is another man's freedom fighter'.[15] The truth behind these words makes it difficult to label a terrorist, and so they are usually classed according to the methods they use – indiscriminate bombings of soft targets, murder, assassinations and other forms of organized crime.

The exact methods employed by terrorists vary between organizations, and there are hundreds of such organizations in the world. They target and recruit weak-willed individuals and use 'sleepers', people that are recruited and trained, but not activated until years later. They are drawn from all levels of society, from white-collar executives to powerful political figures. The risk of terrorism is very real, with increased activity targeting public places, transportation, oil lines, media, stations, military installations, hotels and airports.

What makes a terrorist?
Some people seem born to be terrorists. They have been brought up with the ideals and beliefs of their social environment, they have never felt unconditional love, and they are filled with hatred and anger. Consequently, they are prepared to do anything it takes to achieve their objectives, even suicide.

Revenge can be another factor in the making of a terrorist, as most individuals who choose to fight for a cause in this manner, do so out of revenge for their beliefs. This is a powerful, psychological motivation, and it can consume a man's heart and eat into his soul. Terrorists believe that their actions are for the highest good of themselves and their people. They do not recognize that bombings and indiscriminate killing are wrong, and they cannot conceive of any other path to achieve victory.

Terrorists whose objective is purely financial are probably the most difficult group to comprehend, as they rarely kill anyone. Groups that set up kidnappings for monetary gain generally look after their victims well. Nevertheless, this does not mean that we can sympathize with their cause or their actions.

Fanatics are the most dangerous type of terrorist and the ones that cause the greatest problems. They are driven by ideological support for their religion, and they show no mercy when carrying out the tasks allocated. They are usually highly educated people, but they are simultaneously so narrow-minded that they allow no-one to hinder the execution of their heinous plans.

Other terrorists are idealists, often perceived as nothing more than middle-class troublemakers. An example of such a group would be the Bader-Meinhof gang, an organization of left-wing terrorism in Germany during the 1970s. Supposedly fighting for the working class, the group was responsible for many deaths including targets of bodyguards and chauffeurs of the rich and famous.

During the last three years, there has been an expanding catalogue of significant terrorist attacks, as indicated in box opposite.

Improvised Explosive Devices

The greatest threat from the world's terrorist organizations is the threat from explosive devices. The explosives can be divided into two groups of low and high explosive. Low explosives are used as propellants and launched from a great distance, whereas high explosives can self ignite

Significant Terrorist Attacks, 2001-2006 [16]

September 11th 2001 – Al-Qaeda flew two planes into the World Trade Center Twin Towers in New York, killing thousands of innocent people.

May 2002 – Triple bomb attacks in Casablanca, Morocco, targeted a Spanish restaurant, a five-star hotel and a Jewish community centre, killing 45 people.

October 2002 – An attack on a busy nightclub in Bali, Indonesia, killed 202 people, including 26 Britons.

November 2002 – A suicide bombing at an Israeli-owned hotel in Mombasa, Kenya, killed at least 15 people. There was a simultaneous but unsuccessful attempt to shoot down an Israeli tourist charter plane on the same day.

August 2003 – A suicide car bomb exploded outside the lobby of the US-run Marriott hotel in Jakarta, Indonesia, leaving 12 dead.

November 2003 – A series of incidents in Istanbul included attacks against synagogues, HSBC bank and the British Consulate. Three Britons were killed including the Consul General.

Since 2003, serious attacks, including assassinations and suicide bombings against residential compounds in Saudi Arabia left a number of Britons and other foreign nationals dead.

February 2004 – A ferry in the Philippines was set on fire by an explosive device, killing 116 people.

March 2004 – Simultaneous bomb attacks on commuter trains in Madrid left 202 dead.

July 2004 – Suicide bomb attacks near the US and Israeli Embassies and inside the Prosecutor General's office in Tashkent, Uzbekistan.

August 2004, simultaneous blasts downed two commercial

airliners in Russia, and a suicide attack outside a metro station in Moscow killed nearly 100 people. This was preceded by a suicide attack on the Moscow underground in February 2004 that killed over 40 people.

Autumn 2004 – Three British nationals were kidnapped in Afghanistan and Iraq; two of these individuals are missing, presumed dead.

September 2004 – A car bomb exploded outside the Australian Embassy in Jakarta, Indonesia, killing nine people.

October 2004 – Bomb attacks against tourist sites in the Sinai Peninsula in Egypt killed 34 people and injured 159 others.

December 2004 – Gunmen stormed the US Consulate in Jeddah. This was the first attack against a foreign diplomatic mission in Saudi Arabia.

January 2005 – Following a telephone warning, a separatist group in Spain set off a small bomb in a hotel packed with British holidaymakers, injuring two people. The same group was responsible for a number of bombs exploding in Madrid in December 2004 and February 2005.

February 2005 – A number of bombs were detonated in Makati, Manila, and General Santos and Davao cities in Mindanao, killing nine people and injuring over 130 others.

March 2005 – A suicide bomb attack outside a theatre in Doha Qatar killed one British national and injured at least twelve other people.

July 2005 – Bombings on London underground.

Jan 2007 – attempted bombing in London tube lines.

June 2007 – attempted bombings in Glasgow and London

due to environmental factors and cause much more damage. Examples of explosive materials include picric acid, RDX, mercuric fulminate, TNT, C4, nitro glycerin, semtex and plastic explosive.

Improvised explosive devices are the terrorists' main instruments in their violent campaigns. These devices are used in various scenarios:

Vehicle bombs are increasingly used by terrorists (see Box 7). They have an extremely high risk factor, due to the nature of the device and the associated damage. The vehicles can be placed innocuously in densely populated public areas and detonated in various ways. This concealment means that casualties are usually very high, and many innocent civilians suffer.

These attacks involve meticulous planning and precise timing. The terrorists involved in these attacks are committed and well educated, often from respected universities. Their training by terrorist organizations may extend from six months to several years to carry out one successful bombing campaign. Warning calls precede most attacks, though this varies with terrorist groups and their modus operandi.

There are two kinds of car bomb or vehicle improvised explosive device (VIED). The more common is known as vehicle-borne; the other is the under-vehicle IED, a booby-trap car bomb. A VIED comprises a car or van filled with explosive, or it can be a device attached to a car. This is driven to a target area or planted in a target vehicle. It can be detonated in many ways, such as command wire, movement, and radio control or suicide bomber.

Targets are generally high-profile people such as political figures, staff from international corporations and representatives of high office in government. Physical targets could include military headquarters or political buildings, financial centers, bridges or power stations. Terrorists seeking mass casualties, widespread destruction and high publicity often choose 'soft' targets, such as shopping centers and high streets. The bomb at Enniskillen in Ireland, for example, generated very substantial media attention for the bombers.

It is important to be vigilant in all public places. The harder a target seems, the less likely it will be an attractive, easy option for the terrorist. By becoming a hard target, you can certainly reduce the risks.

Terrorists favor car bombs. Often comprising of an improvised explosive/incendiary mixture, the bomb can be constructed at a safe distance from the target. It can also be detonated from a distance, with the exception of the suicide bomber, this suits the professional terrorist. Car bombs can cause a very high level of devastation, and the fragmentation from the blast often does more damage than the explosion. Much depends on the type of device and its immediate environment.

Bombs may also be carried to target areas. From the perspective of the professional terrorist, an explosive device should be easy to build and easy to transport without attracting attention. Carried bombs are usually concealed in a rucksack or sports-holdall or some other form of hand baggage. There are dangers associated with this practice, and in the past terrorists have unintentionally detonated bombs while carrying them.

Use of Vehicle Bombs by Terrorist Groups [17]

A criminal organization in Italy used a device to assassinate an important member of its judicial system. The bomb was a 60-millimetre butane cylinder that was placed inside the vehicle's exhaust pipe. After the engine had been running for 20 minutes, the heat caused it to explode. This very simple device caused a tremendous amount of devastation.

April 1993 – The Provisional IRA's Bishopsgate bomb in London comprised an Iveco tipper truck loaded with homemade explosive. It was driven to the target area and detonated. Exactly how the device was initiated is still disputed.

1993 – The World Trade Centre bomb in New York comprised homemade explosive loaded into a truck. Fortunately, most of the blast went downwards rather than up into the Twin Towers. As the building was reinforced, it withstood the blast more substantially than a building constructed with bricks and mortar.

February 1996 – Provisional IRA's Canary Wharf bomb in London comprised homemade explosive built into a flatbed lorry. It was supposed to go to the tunnel that ran under the River Thames. If the terrorists had achieved their objectives on that day, they would have flooded London.

August 1998 – The Real IRA mass-casualty car bomb at Omagh killed 29, wounded 220, and caused considerable damage to the town centre. It comprised an improvised explosive device that was placed into a Vauxhall car. The vehicle was then driven to the target area and detonated.

September 2001 – In this attack, the terrorists used aircraft full of innocent people as the explosive, detonator and target. This devastation can still be seen from the tragedy that ensued on that fateful day 9/11. I have visited this area and as a sensitive, I could feel and see the souls that remain grounded there.

November 2003 – The bomb attack on the British Consulate in Istanbul in Turkey was a van driven by a suicide bomber. It killed five and wounded many more. A similar method was used in a parallel attack on the HSBC bank in Istanbul. If the terrorists have access to sufficient materials, they may construct an IED suitable for attaching to a heavy goods vehicle. These typically contain more explosive and cause greater damage; the vehicle can also be used as a mortar launching pad, in similar fashion to the mortar attack on Heathrow Airport many years ago.

Counter-measures for Vehicle Bombs

- Fit secure locks and lockable petrol caps.
- Never leave luggage unattended outside the vehicle.
- Never carry other people's luggage or packages unless you have personally checked the contents.
- Keep your vehicle meticulously clean, this ensures that should there be any tampering the chances of detection will be much higher.
- Do not display documents or clothing with corporate insignia in your car. This will confirm to the terrorist that this is indeed the target vehicle.
- Carry a small torch (perhaps on your key ring) with you to check your vehicle after dark.
- Do not illuminate yourself during dark hours. Switch off the courtesy light inside the car.
- Never use a mobile phone or radio near the vehicle as this could be used as the triggering mechanism.
- Park the vehicle in a lockable garage at home and at work. If no garage is available, leave it in a well-lit area where it can be seen by the general public or is under the direct view of CCTV camera systems.
- Never leave your vehicle unlocked. Remember to secure the bonnet and the boot. On returning to your car, do not assume that the car is as safe as when you left it. Carry out an immediate search of the area around the vehicle to ascertain if there has been any tampering.

Conducting a Vehicle Search

This is an important skill to master. If you are liable to work in hostile areas or for corporations that you know are being targeted, searching your vehicle should become a way of life. It should be conducted routinely if your vehicle is used and parked in an area associated with the corporation (or at home). A good vehicle search should take no more than 20-30 minutes. That is not a lot of time if it saves your life.

Exercise judgment on where you search the car, as a hostile party may identify you during this task. Make sure the area is well enough lit to see what you are doing and an area that is out of sight and out of mind. Bearing in mind that some devices can be heat, light or movement sensitive, your search should be conducted as follows:

- Around the outside of the vehicle, look for things out of place such as strings, wire, moved earth and tape. Check for marks on the ground, such as footprints or grease marks.
- Look for signs of forced entry, such as tampering around windows and doors. A good idea is to dust handles lightly with powder, so that any fingerprints will show up.
- Check underneath the vehicle and inside the wheel arches.
- Look inside the vehicle through the windows, checking all areas.
- Open cautiously and check all door linings.
- Once inside, check the seats, the glove box, under the bonnet and inside the boot. Open the boot latches a little to ensure no wires are connected. You should be familiar with the general view of your engine/underside, in order to recognize unfamiliar objects.
- Look under the dashboard for any hanging wires, wires that look new or traces of cut wires.
- Look inside the hubcaps and inspect the exhaust.
- Check petrol cap.
- Disconnect the battery before going any further. Use a telescopic mirror and a torch to search all other areas that are difficult to access.
- Check any tool compartment and remove all opening compartments slowly and cautiously.
- Check all brakes – a favorite target of the terrorist – and look for

clean wires attached to innocent-looking parts.

- Take care to ensure that the vehicle is not moved while conducting the search. If anything suspicious is noted, do not touch, start or move the vehicle. Emergency procedures should be initiated immediately.

Suicide Bombers

The Al-Qaeda terrorists did not invent the tactic of suicide bombing, but they gave it a new meaning and subsequently became the international symbol for suicide bombers. Their attacks of 11 September 2001 launched a new era in terrorism that is set to continue for some time. More recently, it has to be noted that events in Glasgow and London have gave validation to the aforementioned statements. An interesting contrast is that as we control the sales of weaponry or equipment that is conducive to IED's. The terrorists find other methods to create their weapons of mass destruction by utilizing common household and industrial items.

Suicide bombers are not confined to Middle East countries, but have become endemic in all parts of the world. The terrorists have proved that they can reach any location in any country, and they decide what constitutes a legitimate target. Psychological brainwashing conditions suicide bombers to carry out their missions. In the name of their religion, they are prepared to lay down their life for what they believe is a higher good. They believe their martyrdom secures them a guarantee of a place in nirvana, heaven, spirit or whatever their beliefs may promise.

The bombers consist of suicide bombers that strap the device on to their bodies and individuals that drive vehicles containing the device – both kill themselves in the name of their cause. These terrorists have also been known to use innocent children, brainwashed from birth. The bombings generally occur without warning, deliberately taking communities by surprise. The closest thing to a warning comes when you see a vehicle traveling at high speed towards your compound.

Security Measures

How can you guard against the threat posed by vehicle bombs and suicide bombers? A large number of precautions could be adopted:

- Ensure that there is an individual responsible for the security of your area or corporation and that there is close liaison with the local authorities.
- Through education procedures, make employees within your organization aware of the threats and the risks associated with the company.
- Follow the plan as detailed in your organization's security procedures. For example, maintain adequate vehicle access control, carefully vet all personnel and be very alert to unusual or out-of-place elements.
- Consider installing physical barriers such as gates and high fences, depending on the type of establishment. This will keep out all unauthorized personnel and vehicles.
- Ensure that members of security staff are vetted to a high standard.
- Instal CCTV in all high-threat areas, with as much spatial coverage as possible. Cameras should be chosen with care and should be powerful enough to provide detail in facial features.
- At security control points, maintain a strict regime controlling access through identification of personnel and careful checking of all hand luggage. A secure search facility should be set up at a safe distance from the areas that are under risk. This is the first ring of concentric protection.
- Search all vehicles that are permitted to approach your building. Ensure that they are authorized in advance, searched on arrival, and dependent on the risk appraisal, accompanied throughout their visit.
- Cover your windows with blast-resistant film installed by a reputable company. Conduct a survey of the building.

- Ensure that no one arrives unannounced or without an appointment.
- Be aware of the style of clothing as people approach the areas concerned – is it appropriate for the weather conditions?
- A security-awareness educational package should be running at all times via intranet, announcements or local radio.
- Security staff should patrol all areas regularly and they should be trained in the identification of threats. Look out for anyone acting suspiciously, particularly taking photographs of the area. This may seem a harmless pastime but terrorists use this as a way of carrying out general surveillance of a target. They especially use women as intelligence collators.
- Some terrorists conduct dummy runs by leaving vehicles or packages to identify how long it takes for a response. Alternatively, they may use them as decoys to distract attention from another operation. Remember that these people are highly trained.
- Establish and regularly rehearse bomb threat and evacuation drills. Assembly areas for staff must take account of the proximity to the potential threat. Twenty-five meters from a building is usually considered a safe distance, but with the advances in terrorist technology, this figure should be increased tenfold.
- Train your staff on a regular basis and rehearse your security team in the evacuation response and disaster-recovery policy of your company. Ensure that all staff can identify improvised explosive devices and have an awareness of the modus operandi of terrorists and their associates. All employees should be familiar with proce-dures to be initiated on receiving a bomb threat.
- Ensure that your staff do not become overly tired or complacent whilst carrying out these duties. A tired guard may result in many dead people.

You must remember that suicide bombers expect to die, and therefore the lives of others have no meaning or value for them. They must be denied access by imposing a concentric ring of protection around your establishment. Good security procedures from the ground up must be the basis of all levels of protection. If you live or work in an area deemed to be high risk, you must take the stance that 'forewarned is forearmed'. Good intelligence and close liaison with all agencies are essential.

Incendiary Devices

There are many alternative ways that terrorists may blow up people, buildings and vehicles. The choice of device will relate to the task – options would include using mortar, landmine, sea-mine or booby-trap, none of which is necessarily complicated. However, devising effective measures against these threats is difficult and requires a thorough prior appraisal. If you believe that you face such a threat, you should seek counter-terrorism advice from the local police Counter-Terrorism Security Advisor.

Incendiary attacks are more common. They have been focused mostly on economic targets such as shops or industries, particularly within the pharmaceutical industry (often attributed to organizations such as the Animal Liberation Front), and public buildings. Rather than resulting in human casualties, the objective is to cause economic damage and to weaken public confidence. Bear in mind the following:

- Incendiary devices are generally small, to aid concealment, and come in a variety of packaging.
- They ignite rather than explode. Most are designed to ignite when the package is opened.
- Even if they cause substantial financial damage, they can achieve part of their objective by gaining public support.

As with all prevention measures, good housekeeping and an excellent educational program are imperative.

- Most common public areas are impractical to screen, so good CCTV coverage is essential, supported by regular patrols of high-risk areas. Areas containing flammable material, such as furniture and clothing, should be considered priority areas requiring extra precautions.
- Staff should be adequately trained in the identification of incendiary devices and aware of the ease of planting such a device.
- Searches should be conducted during normal daylight hours and hours of darkness. Make such security measures part of your normal daily routine and anti-terrorist precautions.
- Conduct regular checks on fire extinguishers, sprinklers, smoke alarms and fire blankets as part of normal fire safety procedures.

Anyone finding a suspect device should report it immediately to the appropriate authorities, as defined in your corporate security plan. Whether it is incendiary or explosive, it is important to carry out an immediate evacuation. If an incendiary device ignites, you must evacuate the area, as it is possible that more than one device has been planted. Only if it has caused a relatively small fire – and you are confident with the fire-safety equipment – should you attempt to extinguish it.

Bomb Threat Procedures

Bomb warnings are generally made over the phone. Most are hoaxes, though all are taken seriously. Each year, millions of pounds are lost in revenue to false calls. During the Irish republican terrorist campaign, approximately 10,000 bomb threat calls were made in the Greater London area in one year. Of these, 70 were made by terrorists, 10 of which resulted in the actual discovery of a device.[18] A hoax call is a crime. Even if it is ridiculous or unconvincing, it should be reported to the police.

Calls from terrorists fall into two kinds:

- Bomb threats when none has actually been planted. These hoaxes may not be merely malicious, but designed to disrupt, test reactions or divert attention from another operation. If these calls reveal a weakness in response arrangements, this is exploited to maximum effect.
- Bomb threats warning of a genuine device. These may be attempts to avoid casualties, but they also enable the terrorists to blame others if there are casualties. This is also a method of psychological release for the individual or group, allowing them to disassociate from any blame and state that they show compassion for their victims.

Even genuine warnings are frequently inaccurate about where and when a bomb might explode. The information is disinformation and is a part of the terrorist plot.This is a ploy to undermine attempts to thwart the attack, directing attention to different areas and different times.

Staff receiving a bomb threat may not always be those trained and prepared for it. In that case, your staff may be temporarily in a state of shock at the threat, which will be the closest that many people ever come to acts of terrorism. It is prudent to record all calls received, allowing this material to be analyzed later for intelligence purposes.

Be proactive in devising effective security precautions:

- Identify all risks and personnel likely to receive a call about a threat.
- Consult an anti-terrorism expert or local specialist unit.
- Draw up an effective contingency security plan and practice all evacuation procedures on a regular basis.
- Draw up clear instructions and ensure that all staff read and remember the procedures (initiate a compulsory signed document to be returned to the person in charge).
- Train all staff in these procedures and have instructions readily

accessible.

The instructions may include the following advice:

- Stay calm and listen. Obtain as much information as possible. Ask the caller to speak clearly and be precise about location and timing of the device. Try to identify which group this person represents. Most importantly, try to keep him or her talking.
- Install a caller-identification system and record all calls. Allow enough time for calls to be traced.
- Inform the local authorities or your organization's representative designated to liaise with the authorities.
- Ensure that a full transcript of the call can be made available to appropriate personnel. If you cannot record the call, take as many notes as possible, paying attention to the information required.

Evacuation Planning

Rehearse your bomb-threat procedures as part of your evacuation. The purpose of an evacuation procedure is to move the people under threat to a place of safety. An evacuation may take place in response to:

- A direct threat to the building or the staff through an act of terrorism.
- A threat call received elsewhere and notified to you by the police.
- The discovery of a suspect vehicle or suspicious package within the building.

Depending on the circumstances of your building and the nature of the incident, your evacuation may involve the following components:

- Full evacuation outside the building.
- Evacuation of part of the building, for example if the device is small and thought to be confined to one location.

- Full or partial evacuation to an internal safe area.
- Evacuation of all staff except designated searchers.

You should be aware that in any threat warning, the time given for an explosion is unlikely to be accurate. Prepare an evacuation plan in co-operation with the local law enforcement or anti-terrorist unit. Always keep the police, fire brigade, ambulance service and any other appropriate authorities informed of changes to your plan or dates scheduled for rehearsals.

Components of the plan would include:

- Designated routes and exits depending on the device.
- A designated evacuation team, with appropriate jobs for each individual concerned. They should act as marshals during the evacuation phase.
- Alternative safe havens, to act as a fallback in the event that the original cannot be used, if the device has been placed in the evacuation zone.

For incidents that are definitely explosive in nature, the assembly areas should be at least 500 meters from the danger zone. If an incendiary device is discovered, evacuate the immediate area and conduct searches of the whole building. In the event that a suspected item is delivered to the post room, it should be evacuated, as should any other area within a 100-metres radius.

The decision to evacuate will normally be taken by the head of the company or designated representative in charge of disaster recovery. In all instances, the police and other appropriate authorities should be notified. The above guidelines are non-exhaustive, but it is important that you take these preliminary steps.

Invisible assassins – chemical warfare

Nuclear, biological and chemical (NBC) attacks are known as 'invisible assassins'. The nature of these attacks varies and can have a scale of impact beyond imagination. It is possible that an improvised explosive device could harbor biological agents.

The exact nature of an incident may not become apparent until it is too late. Unfortunately, there are very few measures you can take to protect yourself from these events. Nevertheless, in preparation for such as attack:

- It is imperative that all air vents are blocked and closed off. This helps to negate the possibility of further contamination, as air movement can spread the contaminant rapidly.
- Heating and ventilation systems should be shut down and, if available, alternative breathing-apparatus should be used.
- If the event occurs outside of the building then an immediate shutdown should take place.
- Any individual who has been exposed and directly contaminated by any NBC agent should be evacuated immediately to a safe or controlled area. Emergency services should be notified and the area sealed until they arrive.
- Some form of communication should be left in the room to allow calls to be made in the event of further emergencies.
- Ensure that no one is allowed to enter or leave the area until the all clear has been given.

A small radiological device is unlikely to cause immediate ill effects, and people may not realize they have been exposed to it until some time afterwards. In comparison, biological agents may be noticed within a few days, as they are primarily designed for spreading destructive diseases such as anthrax. They operate like a time bomb, the important factors being the incubation period of the organism and the environmental conditions. However, with chemical agents the impact may be immediate or apparent within a few seconds.

The nature and diversity of the materials make it difficult to provide a detailed analysis of nuclear, biological and chemical and indicators, but the following summary highlights the more common warning signals:

- Hazardous warnings on the letter or package.
- Unexpected granular, crystalline or finely powdered material – the color is can be varied and disguised.
- Unexpected sticky substances, sprays or vapors or unpleasant smells – but some agents are odorless.
- Stains or dampness on the packaging, and irritation on areas of the body immediately on contact with the package/substance.

Unlike improvised explosive devices, NBC agents can be activated just by touching the package or by being close to it. If the contents are in powdered, crystalline or liquid form, it may require no initiator other than the air that you breathe.

Any suspect item should be taken seriously, but most will be false alarms, and a few may be hoaxes. Try to make your procedures effective but not needlessly disruptive. At all times, remain vigilant and treat every incident as real. Remember that terrorists get closer every day to deploying these weapons of mass destruction.

Postal Bomb Recognition

A postal bomb is usually designed to explode at the moment of opening. The device will invariably contain an explosive charge, a detonator/igniter to initiate the charge, and some form of triggering mechanism. A postal bomb can be incendiary or biological.

The sender of an improvised explosive device will go to great lengths to ensure that it will not be detected or to minimize the risk of detection. The envelope will look innocent, the address will be professional in appearance, and the recipient will identify it as a known source. A mail worker's ability to identify suspect packages relates directly to the level of training received. The following list contains a number of tips on characteristics of suspect packages:

- Unknown point of origin.
- Unusual address label, perhaps containing spelling errors.
- Uneven balance to the package.
- Very heavy package for its size.
- Unusual smell or greasy prints on the packaging – this is an indicator of plastic explosive.
- Springiness in the top, bottom or sides of the package or letter – do not bend it excessively.
- Wires protrude from it.
- It generates a ticking noise.
- A hole (like a pinhole) in the package wrapping or envelope – another indicator of explosive, which needs to breathe or will otherwise become ineffective.
- A smell of almonds or marzipan.
- It is thought to contain something that is not expected.
- The flap of the envelope is stuck down completely – there is usually a gap at each end of the gummed flap.

There are other, more specific indicators to consider when examining letters:

- A bomb will probably have stiffening by cards or metal, and not only folded paper inside the envelope. Use your intuitive ability, and your mind will alert you before anything else will.
- Letters usually weigh up to 28 grams. Postal bombs will usually weigh more than 56 grams and therefore need more than the usual postage stamps. They will tend to be unusually thick and are likely

to feel lopsided.

- If an envelope or package arrives with another envelope or package inside, be cautious when examining or put it in though an X-ray machine.
- Explosives are very rarely solid. It may not be possible to feel solid objects within the package – most explosive devices and associated packages will feel very flexible.

The act of opening a postal bomb usually causes the explosion. These simple tasks can initiate the device:

- Tearing the envelope open.
- Pulling out a tucked-in envelope flap.
- Using a paperknife.
- Removing the contents of an already opened envelope.

If you have diligently carried out everything above, and yet you are still suspicious, place the suspect package on a flat surface. Leave the area and evacuate if necessary in accordance with your security policy. Ensure all windows are open and seal the area. Contact the police for further assistance.

- Do not touch the package in any way.
- Do not take the package to the Security Officer.
- Do not put it in a bucket of water or sand.
- Do not bend or flex the package.
- Do not operate electrical emissions equipment such as radios or mobile phones within 25 meters of the suspect device.

PART 3 INTUITION

10: SECURITY AND THE PSYCHIC SENSE

Could 9/11 have been prevented?

Consider the following scenario relating to the terrorist attacks on the United States of America. Assume that a high percentage of people have accessed the power of the spirit available to everyone. Imagine that I am an executive and that I work in the World Trade Center. I wake up every morning at 5.30am, eat a light breakfast, and I leave at 7am to make my journey to work. However, on September 11th, I wake up feeling out of sorts, experiencing an unfamiliar awareness. Maybe I have had a bad dream. For the first time in 20 years, I call in sick. I watch the news a little later on ... and you know the rest.

On that fateful day, I manage to escape death, but why? The universe in its infinite wisdom saves me by giving me signs, warnings through various senses, and my interpretation results in a change of mind that ultimately saves my life. This is the development of awareness on a higher level of consciousness, boosting the inner senses. If we can all raise our awareness to understand those inner senses, then disasters such as the 9/11 catastrophe might in some way be averted or significantly reduced in scale.

Is it possible to become a psychic anti-terrorist? Yes of course. From even simple cases of utlilising intuitive ability to prevent simple less drastic dangers of life- we can learn to utlise that same intuition to prevent us from acts of terror. It is done with the same divine gifts of the spirit. Amplification of those gifts will most certainly be stronger as the universe in its infinite designing wisdom will be trying to warn you of the impending danger. Dreams will be clearer and may involve frightening signs, synchronicity of events and warnings will be clearer. Clairvoyant images will be stronger and involve strong gut feelings that stir your soul.

Ireland's Eye

I once worked on a case that involved investigating criminal activity in Scotland and Ireland. During my intelligence gathering phase I had mediocre success in identifying ringleaders and arranging meetings to arrange elements of business that they were interested in. I knew that what I was doing was dangerous to myself and yet knowing that I was working for a higher good of all gave me confidence. I always trusted in a higher power and also knew that I was covered by a higher authority in the country I was working.

I had managed to arrange a meeting in Ireland, the time and date was arranged. I was to meet the head of one of the organisations. I was to fly over, get picked up at the airport and taken to a bar that they frequented to conduct business. Two days before I was due to fly and that night, I had a dream. In my dream I was gagged and all was dark, I could not breathe and I heard unfriendly voices. The next day I kept having bad visions. The universe had given me the signs I required in order to remain safe. I later found out that it was intended by the criminals I was investigating that I was never to return from that trip and would have been shot.

Intuitive warnings

If we look at the above case, you will see that I used several gifts of the spirit; clairvoyance, clairaudience and clairsentience. These gifts ensured that I would live to work another day. These intuitive warnings showed up in various ways, by sight, hearing and feelings. These are also the same senses that you can develop to ensure your survivability in an ever changing dangerous environment. Being able to understand this language is irrefutable in knowing that what you see is what you feel and what you feel is your intuition. That feeling will save your life.

Windows of opportunity

In every given situation, 'windows of opportunity' exist. By existing, I mean they are alive, like life in the fifth and sixth dimensions of spiritual understanding of mind, body and spirit, and there is no beginning and no end. The fifth and sixth dimensions are the levels of spirit beyond the physical senses. You need to absorb these important concepts. From case histories, it is evident that those who survive the gravest of situations exploit windows of opportunity or a paradox in time. In non-technical language, this refers to a point during an attack or other situation when an element of weakness or relaxation reveals itself. By training your mind through daily meditation to recognize these windows of opportunity, you will perceive features that relieve you of the danger that exists in this inconsistency of time. Meditating makes you more aware and therefore your awareness is far superior, allowing you to recognize subtle changes in energy and to exploit the opportunities within.

Put more simply, imagine if someone grabs you or tries to choke you. There is a point when, in order to carry out the intention to its maximum level, the mind has to relax to send signals to the brain to carry out the next move. When the muscles of the physical body relax to initiate this next stage, the conscious mind signals this move by thought. This is your window of opportunity for survival. If you have increased your awareness, then you will sense the changes in energy, and the subtle movements of the muscular action of the perpetrator will seem far stronger. In this instance, you must move and act quickly utilizing all of your will to protect yourself. Perhaps you will be able to change the balance of the opponent and escape or strike quickly and land a debili-tating blow to your attacker.

Remote perception

Remote perception is the phrase coined by Dale Graff that encompasses the use of all psychic senses. Remote viewing is the generic term used to describe the abililty of a psychic to tune into target areas and sketch or describe what they are viewing. Time and distance are no limiting factor. Remote perception viewers have the ability to track down fugitives who are on the run or locate abducted individuals. It is also possible to use remote viewing to locate missing objects or stolen goods, which can assist law enforcement agencies. As our shift into spiritual awareness moves closer, so to does the chance of utilizing spiritual gifts to aid law enforcement and intelligence agencies in the fight against crime.

Perhaps we can take remote viewing a little further within our own perceptiveness. Not bound to use this ability for Intelligence purposes; we can utilize remote viewing to look into the immediate future and perceive any possible obsticles. Allow me to use the following example. Say for instance that you have decided to take small trip away somewhwhere - even for the day. Take a little time to meditate and move into your quiet space, ask the universe to show you in your minds eye, any possible problems that may manifest on or before your journey. Perhaps during your meditation you experience a vision of a severe car accident. This could mean a no of things and not necessarilly that you will be involved in one. It could mean that you will be delayed considerably due to a severe accident or it could be something that is different to your own understanding and perception.

Law enforcement and intuition
There have been many instances where agents of intelligence agencies and officers of local law enforcement have called on the services of individuals with special gifts. The use of psychic investigators is a secret that most agencies will never admit to, yet thanks to the thirst of the media and the odd intuitives' search for fame, it has become reported and has become a more widely acceptable field. Using psychic investigators allows agencies to open new avenues of intelligence.It has now come to light that intelligence organisations such as MI5, CIA, the FBI and other law enforcement partners are using psychics more and more. Operation STARGATE of which Dale Graaf was the project director, is one prime example of governemnts using individuals for remote viewing to gain intelligence on targetted installations. Dale's book, *Tracks in the psychic wilderness* Is an exhaustive account of his work in this field. Uri Geller

has been used by the CIA for investigations into remote viewing. Joseph McMoneagle was one of the managers and an active operator of project STARGATE, his book, *Memoirs of a Psychic Spy* is a tremendous eye opener to the workings of this operation. Another renowned American medium to help the FBI in murder enquiries is Norreen Renier. She has also lectured to new recruits at the FBI academy on the merits of using psychic investigators. These are some quotes from her site by FBI agents:

"Noreen never could have known this stuff beforehand and she was so accurate it was chilling." — R. Krolak (Retired Lt. Commander)
"She helped to locate a plane containing the body of a relative of an FBI agent." — Robert Ressler (Ex-FBI)

Kuwait was predicted

An operative from a government remote viewing project acurately predicted the military strike in Kuwait. Remote viewers from project STARGATE decided to target their efforts on Sadaam Hussein. Their task was to tune into Sadaam himself and identify his plans and intentions. During the time they were viewing they were able to pick up not only his intentions, but what he is like as a person, his likes, dislikes and those that were attached to him. As you can imagine that type of intelligence is excellent. The only problem was that you cannot mobilise a whole military force on the strenghth of psychic vibes. However, as we change in our perceptions, perhaps one day we will be able to use our abilities to stop situations such as these.

It is possible that with remote viewing, it is not just working clairvoyantly to see images of installations or military bases. By utilizing the other psychic senses can we predict dates of events or imminent attacks?

Kidnapping and the psychic

If inevitably kidnapping cannot be prevented, psychic mediums can help in locating the kidnap victim. One of the many operations of STARGATE was to locate kidnap victims and the project's successes have been documented. Dale Graff, the project director, details this in his book *Tracks in the Psychic Wilderness*. Psychic mediums are able to tune into the subtle vibrations of the kidnap. At the beginning of this book, I explained how events leave an emotional trail of energy. That energy, as you can imagine, is even stronger during a kidnap – fear will be getting stronger. A good psychic medium should be able to tune into evidence of where the captive may be, the surrounding area and the local landmarks. This increases the chances of survival for the kidnap victim and aids the authorities in taking the appropriate action.

Psychic investigators

Many mediums are being called to help with those investigations, and many a skeptic has been dumfounded by the information transferred by a psychic investigator. Whilst we were in the USA, my wife and I assisted in a missing person case and the officer in charge was a skeptic. The only reason that he allowed us to help was because he had spent time in the UK and knew some of the units I had worked with. A young woman had gone missing and we were asked if she was still alive and what had taken place surrounding her disapearance. It was very challenging to do it in front of someone who did not belief it was possible to find useful information this way. We told him that she was still alive and said she would return home. We later called back to see how things were going and voila! the young lady returned home exactly as predicted and the evidence was validated. To this day, the officer is confused about how we knew – yet he keeps us on his books for future reference.

Certainly, there are psychics out there who document cases to create their own fame. The media publicize this, recognizing the thirst for knowledge and examples of the paranormal. The psychic is not there to solve cases. The psychic medium is only there to offer intelligence that could not be gathered by normal means. The psychic is able to tune into the subtle vibrations that surround objects and people. This will promote clairvoyant or psychic images that may offer the investigators another avenue to follow. If a case becomes a homicide investigation, it is not unusual for the deceased spirit to communicate with the medium to help the investigation.

Jo and I worked on a case in the highlands of Scotland that had been unsolved for 30 years. There was so much controversy surrounding the case and many psychics and mediums had tried to get involved for their own gane. On arriving in the Highlands in 2007 we were interviewed by the Newspaper for our work that we were doing. After the innitial press interest the paper contacted us again and asked us if we would investigate the Rennie Macrea murder. At this stage, i must enforce that we do not get involved in any cases unless we are asked to do so by official sources. The paper investigated our findings and checked out our credability, the story was front page news and centre spread news. We had come closest to offering some kind of acceptable explanation for the murder and the paper had reflected this in their story. The best that could have been achieved with this particular case was to offer closure to family members.

Evidence for the sixth sense

Beyond the five senses of hearing, sight, touch, smell and taste, some individuals are able to use a sixth sense. This higher sense is the gifts of the spirit innate in all of us and has many different facets such as clairvoyance (seeing), clairaudience (hearing), clairsentience (feeling), and claircognizance (knowing).

Skeptics who irrefutably deny the existence of a paranormal, psychic or spiritual ability, dismiss the evidence for it. Could this denial be based in a fear of the unknown – the fear of not being able to believe what we cannot perceive with our physical senses? If we do not understand something, it is normal to fear it. Stone Age humans feared fire. Why did they fear it? Because they had no understanding of it, and when they used it wrongly, they hurt themselves. This is the same as psychic phenomena – we do not understand it or its potential, and if we use it wrongly it can be extremely dangerous.

Since the dawn of the spiritual movement there have been people who have studied evidence for the sixth sense or the ability to commune with those in another dimension and tried to explain it scientifically. Modern scientists such as Gary Schwartz, Rupert Sheldrake, David Fontana, Dale Graff, Bruce Moen, Archie Roy, Dean Radin and Harry Oldfield have tirelessly examined and researched to gain an insight into life after death and psychic or paranormal ability. They have collected thousands of case studies and carried out blind, double blind and triple blind tests to prove the existence of the sixth sense, and measures were taken to ensure that no trickery was involved. The subjects had no prior knowledge of the tests before or during the events. Fraud was not in the equation – the results speak for themselves.

Many years ago, cartographers and philosophers were of the opinion the world was flat and square. The thought that an individual could believe the world was round was absurd. Of course, one such individual raised his head above the parapet to claim the truth and prove that it was indeed round. The skeptics laughed and jeered claiming that Christopher Columbus was not a man of sound mind. We know the outcome of his travels; he did prove the world was round and stumbled on new continents during his travels. Maybe one day the scientific evidence collected by eminent scientists will undoubtedly prove our belief in the sixth sense. Even the noted skeptic James Raandi cannot refute that the world is round.

There are two kinds of evidence for the sixth sense: personal experience and the science-based. Never before has there been such controversy in the science world, between scientists of a materialistic persuasion and those scientists of a psychological persuasion who study behavioral science.

Sigmund Freud – the closet psychic
The world-renowned psychiatrist Dr Sigmund Freud supported the claims

of psychic ability and discussed it in papers that were only available to his inner circle. He was cautious in his approach and support for this new science because of the ridicule that he would receive from his closed-minded peers. He stated:

> "There is little doubt that if attention is directed to occult phenomena, the outcome will very soon be that occurrence of a number of them will be confirmed, and it will probably be a long time before an acceptable theory covering these new facts can be arrived at. But the eagerly attentive onlookers will not wait so long. At the very first confirmation, the occultists will proclaim the triumph of their views. They will be hailed as liberators from the burden of intellectual bondage; they will be joyfully acclaimed by the credulity lying ready to hand since the infancy of the human race and the childhood of the individual. There may follow a fearful collapse of critical thought, of determinist standards and of mechanistic science." (Rhine 1937, p115)

Nowadays there is evidence that his prediction is coming to fruition, though many skeptics – no matter how convincing the evidence, still do not believe the research and strive to refute it. They will need to personally experience a full materialization of a spirit to believe in extra sensory view.

Scientific evidence

The closest a scientist ever has to prove the existence of a super sense, or sixth sense, as it is commonly known, is the revered biologist, Rupert Sheldrake. In his latest book *The Sense of Being Stared At* he documents many experiments that he and his research associates have carried out. He likens some of the psyche or intuitive ability to that of animal behavior and their seeming ability to predict events. This seems due to their heightened sensitivity and poses the question whether our extra sensory ability is normal rather than paranormal (out of the norm).

Maybe you have experienced sitting at home and thinking of someone you know, then suddenly the phone rings and the person at the other end is the same person who was in your thoughts. Is this coincidence or synchronicity?

Mediumship

Mediumship has been around for thousands of years; hence, humankind has had a need to research the concept and test the boundaries of science to prove the existence of life after death. Organizations such as The Monroe Institute have been involved with exploring the human consciousness, and continuing the research after the physical death of the body. The Monroe Institute believes that our consciousness holds the keys to experiences of human existence. To understand our consciousness can change our destiny in a more intensely spiritual manner.

Gary E Schwartz PhD is professor of psychology, medicine, neurology, psychiatry and surgery at the University of Arizona and director of its Human Energy Systems Laboratory and is the author of *The Afterlife Experiments* and is the co-author with Linda G Russek PhD of *The Living Energy Universe*. After receiving his doctorate from Harvard University, he served as a professor of psychology and psychiatry at Yale University, director of the Yale Psychophysiology Center, and co-director of the Yale Behavioral Medicine Clinic. He has published more than 400 scientific papers, and 11 academic books.

Dr Schwartz has tested some of the world's best-known mediums including John Edward and Allison Dubois. To my mind there is no better evidence than the papers and results from his tests, which are described in *The Afterlife Experiments*. Other studies can be found on the Veritas website www. veritas.arizona.edu/index.htm.

His tests have been rigorously conducted, controls were in place with no possibility of cold readings as suggested by many skeptics or mind reading as suggested by Derren Brown in his book *Tricks of the Mind*. The results speak for themselves, though the conclusions may be out of the reach of closed minds that have closed the doors to their own consciousness. Investigations into human consciousness continue to research evidence of life after death and the existence of the sixth sense.

Mediumship can also be used for protection

Everyone has the ability to communicate with spirit, and from the dawn of time there have been instances of visitations from another realm - warning the receiver of immediate danger. Even within scriptures in all religions are tales and evidence of heavenly visitations from the angelic realms or other spiritual beings. If it is not someone's time to pass on from this earthly existence and an event occurs to expedite the departure. An angel has the ability to intervene where necessary and thwart the early departure. There have been many instances whereby deceased relatives have visited individuals to warn them of impending danger. The result of this warning has inevitably saved the individual from disaster.

In contrast, that little voice that you hear within your own mind is also a form of mediumship. It is just as effective a warning system than receiving the materialization of a spirit being, which in most instances would scare the life from you anyway. Meditation is the key to developing this side of you which is innate in every one of us.

Scientific explanation

In *The Sense of Being Stared At* (Arrow books 2003) Rupert Sheldrake explains these kinds of events in the context of a new way of looking at matter and energy. He epitomizes this in the statement "Matter is no longer the fundamental reality, as it was for old-style materialism. Fields and energy are now more fundamental than matter. The supreme particles of matter have become vibrations of energy within fields. The boundaries of scientific 'normality' are shifting again with a drawing recognition of the reality of consciousness. The powers of the mind, until now ignored by physics, are the new scientific frontier." Could I have picked up the information by tuning into that mass consciousness of energy?

Sheldrake has tested thousands of individuals on sixth sensory living and the sense of being stared at and his evidence has been compiled into various papers and books worldwide. For many years, many of his professional colleagues dismissed his scientific approach, yet now years later and with far more evidence, he has become a world-renowned lecturer and speaker at scientific conferences worldwide.

As a specialist in security and esoteric arts, I particularly resonated with Sheldrake's hypothesis on the sense of being stared at. There have been many examples documented in his work of individuals knowing that they were being watched or stared at from a distance. One such example of this was that of a friend of mine, who was an undercover agent who worked with me on many operations. One particular operation we were involved in warranted covert surveillance on a target in central London, and Europe for a blue-chip company. The target was stealing trade secrets from the company and had managed to coerce others into starting a separate company. Some of these individuals had very high-level connections in world financial institutions. They had stolen economic models that had bearing on the world economy. My partner situated himself in an excellent position where he had perfect sight on the target at his office premises in London. The distance from the target to the surveillance post was at least 400 yards, and the target could not have possibly known that we were there. After we finished our stint, we returned to our hotel and evaluated the evidence. The target had looked direct into the lens of the camera on more than one occasion, but he could not have possibly seen the camera from that distance. Looking into the camera would suggest that, in alignment with Sheldrake's theory, he felt he was being watched.

Sheldrake discusses many examples and supports them with scientific evidence. From his research, many other scientists who are Newtonian in their belief (Sir Isaac Newton's theory of mass atomic distribution) are beginning to change their mind-set.

Try this for yourself the next time you are watching someone. Maybe you will be on a bus or public transport. Choose your target carefully and send thoughts to them with your mind, staring in their direction. You will be amazed at the response – note it down and carry out your own experimentation. Your target will normally turn around and look in your direction or perhaps start to feel a little uncomfortable. Ensure that you carry out this experiment carefully and do not upset anyone – especially those of the opposite sex.

Precognitive Dreams

Now let's consider the effectiveness of precognition to avert potential disasters. Many a sensitive claims to have predicted the disaster of September 11th 2001 by dreaming about the event. Some individuals vividly dreamt about buildings blowing up or planes crashing into buildings. These dreams were experienced before the event and ultimately saved the lives of the individuals that experienced them.

One evening last year I had a very vivid dream about attacks on London. I was in a street and on top of a roof on a high building in London. I saw people running around frantically, consumed by fear and terror. Sirens playing their high-pitched sounds raced to the scene and many people lay injured with blood on their faces. I saw men walking away laughing and feeling happy about their achievements. My dream detailed targets that terrorists would try to blow up. Several days later two bombs went off in London and many were injured. The dream left me very upset but the universe uses our dream state to warn us of potential dangers – to give us answers to potential problems that we experience and to facilitate healing within our energy fields. Dreams are an important life saving and life-giving facet of our spiritual make up.

Several individuals had incredibly disturbing dreams before the attacks of 9/11 and because of those dreams, they stayed at home. Others had daydreams that were disturbing, and became upset and missed their transport to work. I am sure that many of you that are reading this book have, at some point in your lives, experienced dreams of a precognitive nature.

Here's another scenario. Let's say that you wake up in the morning and prepare yourself for the usual long journey on a commuter train. However, something deep within you tells you that perhaps you should not go today – a strong feeling that makes you decide not to travel. Perhaps you've had a dream that disturbed you on an emotional level, and you feel you just can't face going in to work. Later in the day, you watch the television news and learn to your horror, the train you normally catch has de-railed or was targeted for criminal attack, resulting in many deaths and many more injuries. What told you not to go that morning? Why are you still alive when others are dead? What gave you that hunch? It is your in-built warning system, your intuition. Learning to use that intuitive ability will stop you being a target or becoming another statistic.

Lucid dreaming

Scientists such as Dale Graff have explored the phenomena of dreaming to link PSI to sleep and to examine its use in remote viewing. The practicable applications of lucid dreaming are immense and can be used to benefit society in several ways. In an experiment conducted by Dale, he used a renowned remote viewer to sense particular problems on a canoe journey that he and his colleagues had taken. During the journey, Dale and his colleagues ran into some problems along the way. The remote viewer correctly identified the problems in his dream and recorded them in his journal for validation later. On each stage of the journey, the viewer correctly identified the geography of the target area and the emotions of the target individual. This type of dream viewing offers an exploration into remotely viewing the location of expeditions in trouble or of individuals that are lost. It has a tremendous application, not just for law enforcement and intelligence personnel, but also to search and rescue teams all over the world. What if we could harness this ability for use in such natural disasters as the tsunami in Asia to find missing individuals or people who were in trouble?

Dale also noted there was a connection between telepathic calls of senders and receivers in situations that required immediate responses. When someone is in dire need and their life is in danger, subconsciously the person in trouble will be sending out distress messages from their subconscious. Spirit could also have a hand in this by alerting the person most useful to help. No matter which method is used, there is a mind-to-mind connection that alerts the receiver to the request for help. This has been proven by the experimentation of such scientists as Dale Graff, Rupert Sheldrake and Harry Oldfield.

Consider that you are out on an expedition and you cannot contact civilization because of having deficient equipment; if you ran into trouble – what would you do? Could you send a telepathic message for help to a particular receiver? This is entirely possible as just such an experiment was achieved during Dale Graff's research.

Dreams can reveal answers to questions. In this book I discuss the use of using our gifts to investigate cold cases – normally murder. In the next chapter I detail the case investigated for a newspaper in the highlands of Scotland. They asked my wife and I to investigate a cold case. During the investigation and our meditations, we gained lots of relevant information. However, during my sleep time, I received an exceptionally lucid dream that answered further questions that we had of the case. This dream appeared in the centre pages of the *Highland News*;

"In the dream I saw Renee and she was showing me a large house. She said the house was significant and she showed me a long, straight road with woods and banks on either side. She told me to watch as the road turned into molten lava, burning everything in sight."

Jock recalled: "I remember turning round and saying to her 'Why is this happening?' and she said 'Now, watch'. The house crumbled and just fell in and everything was disappearing into the lava and being consumed."

The above is an example of how the power of dreams from the universe can answer questions that ultimately could never be answered by human consciousness or humanistic methods. In our dream state we continually live on another higher plane of existence.

CHAPTER 11: THE SIXTH SENSE

When you have overcome your fear, you are calm. When you are calm, you can exercise awareness. When you are aware, you can listen to your sixth sense, your intuition. Only then are you really alive!!!

By unlocking your sixth sense, you can become your own bodyguard and personal adviser. You will listen to yourself before you do anything, and your mind and body will give you the answer or show you how to protect yourself. Listening to your intuition will save your life.

Most people have had experiences such as walking into a bar or a building where there has been a disturbance and the atmosphere seems charged. Your body and your mind will usually give you some indication that this place is not safe and you should leave. This is not as difficult to explain as you might think. Every fuelled situation leaves an emotional trail of energy, and we instinctively tune in to that frequency. Your hair may stand on end and you may feel shivers. Many people will put this down to a psychosomatic symptom of the mind, but in fact you are using your natural intuitive ability and your body and spirit is warning you off. It is up to you to pay attention to this warning. An uncomfortable emotional feeling is akin to an alarm, yet through our own ignorance and machismo, we would rather ignore it for fear of feeling week.

What is the sixth sense?
Intuitive ability is a skill that we all have, and it was granted to us even before we were born. However, social pressures and religious doctrines subdue it and keep it restrained. Only occasionally does this natural ability surface, and then it usually shocks us to the core. If we awaken to the knowledge that intuition is there for us, that we can bring it back from the depths of our soul, we could use this ability to protect us and help us move forward in life, knowing that we are supported by the universe. In order to use our intuition we must remain grounded and ensure that we do

not live in our minds; intuition surrounds us every day, but we miss its simple signals.

An analogy of this would be when you are traveling down a main highway and you spot the sign that tells you in which way to go. Yet if you miss it, you will inevitably get lost. It is so easy to miss our signs and signals even when we are aware that they are there. One little diversion and you can miss the sign entirely. The universe, in its infinite wisdom will not lay out your fate or destiny to one sign; instead there will be a plethora of little subtle signs that will gently guide you on your right path. By remaining aware to the universe and its wisdom, we become acutely aware of the signs around us.

No matter what your belief is, intuition comes in many forms. It is only when you accept all religions, beliefs and creeds, that you can develop fully in the world of spirit. There are no boundaries – nothing is entirely right or wrong. How many prophets and mystics have been able to understand what spirit was trying to say? We all have the gifts of the spirit within. Intuition is within us all and is known as many things:

- Gut Instinct
- Spirit within
- Intuition
- Feelings
- Sixth Sense
- Vibes
- Inner Knowing
- Inner Perception

Dream-state precognition

In all traditions, religions and in all walks of life, dreams have been used to predict the future or to provide answers to important questions. Ancient seers have been courted to provide answers to royalty and commanders about all aspects of battles or outcomes of all dealings within court. Some rulers made decisions on controlling their kingdom based on what the seer or prophet said they could see with the inner sight.

Dreams are part of our inner inheritance and have always been a focus for every living society – from the Aborigines of Australia to societies in Europe and America. In early Egypt and Middle Eastern society, they relied on dreams for insight into life and especially in Egypt; dreams were used for healing concerns. Hundreds of healing temples were built by the Greek civilization to promote dream healing. Nowadays some intuitive individuals are adept at using dreams to gain insight into the soul of an individual, or to scan the body to discover problems within the physiology.

Dreams do not have to be restricted to sleep; we can achieve a dream state in waking hours. This is normally recognized as 'daydreaming' and though some think that daydreaming is just a person's ability to fantasize, it can hold answers to the many problems we face in life. If we only recognized that daydreaming is an integral part of our connection to our spiritual nature. It allows us to use our clairvoyant gifts.

With all the gifts that we have at our disposal, it is obvious through trial and error that we can enhance our ability to protect ourselves from danger now or in the future. Maybe that element of our daydream could warn us of potential disaster or in that dream state we could receive messages that alert us to the emergency help needed by a loved one.

Perhaps you could be walking down a particular street in your neighborhood and your daydream changes from a nice one, to one that is particularly upsetting. There would be no conscious reasoning for this sudden change in emotion. This would be spirit alerting you to problems that may be ahead, that may be hazardous to your safety. What would you do? Would you ignore the fact that you had a nice vision and then suddenly it turned into one that was not pleasant? On the other hand, would you heed the warning and increase your awareness – thus increasing your survivability.

Dreams can also be used effectively to find out answers to puzzling questions. Before giving a reading I will ask the universe to show me what I need to know for that person, the evening before. In most instances, I will have a dream that will correspond to that individual's concerns at the time, then, when it comes to doing the reading, I am armed with some of the information.

My wife and I were once asked to investigate a murder case that remained unsolved for over 30 years in the highlands of Scotland. We were asked by the newspaper in that area, and after much convincing and soul searching we agreed. We had no information on the case and the little we had was where we began. We went to the area that events occurred to pick up on the residual psychic energy that was there. It was not long before we started to receive information, and the information we were receiving did not concur with the opinions of everyone else.

We decided to go home and meditate on the case to attempt some form of communication with the victim. During the meditation, my wife channeled some very important information regarding the case and that night I had an amazing lucid dream that not only confirmed the info that my wife had gained but also added more to the case. During the dream, the victim came to me and told me of the events that had occurred that led to her passing and why it had remained unsolved for so many years. She also made a revelation as to the confession that would be made in a passing. Our information was collaborated and found to be the closest to some kind of truth. The paper ran the story and it was front page news as well as centre pages. They had ensured that we were as they quoted "The real deal" before running the story. The story offered a form of closure for members of the family, and for the police; it allowed further intelligence from which they can investigate should they so wish.

The Information that we received came in the form of a lucid dream and a daydream and was checked by the individuals concerned to be the closest to the truth. Many psychics worked in this case and as quoted by the newspaper – all were dismissed as fantasy but we were found to be accurate and genuine (The Highland News 2007). This story is a prime example of how a dream can act not only as a precognitive warning, but can aid in putting closure to events from the past. This is due to the residual energy held in the universe and the direct communication with spiritual energy.

Aura – your personal energy field

We all have a vibration field, an energy that surrounds every one of us that holds our personal model of life. This field consists of electromagnetic particles that resonate at a particular vibration and frequency. Scientists have been researching this energy field for a long time, yet it remains at the fringe of scientific acceptance. In the last few years, well-known scientists such as Harry Oldfield and Dr Barbara Brennan have broken through that barrier to try proving and explaining the existence of the auric field.

The aura phenomenon has been around for thousands of years and can be credited to the haloes seen in the iconic paintings of religious figures. In ancient religions and shamanic teachings as with new age science, it is believed that the aura is made up of electromagnetic particles. The existence of this magnetic field in living and non-living objects has been demonstrated through Kirlian photography. This type of photography was invented by [19]Simyon Kirlian who in 1939 accidentally discovered that if an object on a photographic plate is subjected to a strong electric field, an image is created on the plate.

Kirlian made controversial claims that his method showed proof of spiritual auras, said to resemble an outline of the object like a colorful halo surrounding the living object. An experiment advanced as evidence of energy fields produced by living entities, involves taking Kirlian contact photographs of a leaf from a plant at set periods. Its gradual withering has been credited to the theory the decline in the strength of the *aura* is the cause of the death of the leaf. Many individuals are able to see these energy fields and vouch that the color seems to change when the individual is nearing physical death.

Barbara Brennan is an ex-NASA physicist and author of *Hands of Light and Light Emerging*. She has been investigating the phenomena of healing through the human energy field for many years, and is now the head of a worldwide healing modality. She has pragmatically proven through her research that health and disease is in direct correlation to the make up of the human energy field or the aura.

How do you think she knew about the aura before she started to study and carry out further scientific tests? Obviously as a NASA physicist, she was well versed in physics and other scientific theories. The first instance of this was when she began to perceive this aura with her own physical eyes. This sparked off her interest and even when she closed her eyes or looked away from the aura, she could still perceive it. Over a period of 15 years and through meditation she was able to distinguish the various fields of the aura more vividly because of the expanding of her consciousness. In the beginning, Barbara Brennan remained incredibly skeptical and yet through the expansion of her own levels of consciousness she destroyed that belief system.

One important quote from her book *Hands of Light* (Bantam) is: "I saw that the energy field is intimately associated with a person's health and well-being. If a person is unhealthy, it will show in the energy field as an unbalanced flow of energy and or stagnated energy that has ceased to flow and appears as darkened colors. In contrast, a healthy person shows bright colors that flow easily in a balanced field. These colors and forms are very specific to each illness."

With practice and time, we can learn to open up our psychic centers and receive inbound information in many ways using all psychic abilities. These centers when balanced and unblocked can be an effective method of protecting the mind, body and spirit.

How is the aura viewed?

As evolution changes the way in which we perceive things, so has science changed with the evolution of man. Now with that change in science we are able to view the aura. Scientists such as Harry Oldfield have invented equipment that pictures the aura in real-time. A leap in scientific research in this field is changing the way we look at our own existence.

Dr Harry Oldfield is a scientist and inventor famed for his invention of the photo imaging system that reveals the human energy field or aura. This has become known as PIP, Polycontrast Interference Photography. His research and development has successfully produced equipment that allows the visual presentation on computer interfaces of the human energy field.

He has managed to use the natural energy of crystals to help with the image enhancement of microscopes and instruments. Now individuals can easily see the human energy field and perceive what intuitive people have been seeing for thousands of years. He has pioneered non-invasive complementary therapy and has only recently been accepted by the controversial scientific community. His work is changing the way we deal with healing. *http://www.electrocrystal.com/*

Like many an innovator before him, Harry Oldfield has often found himself on 'the fringe' of science. However, his recent work has become acceptable in scientific circles. This work uses Harry Oldfield's ideas about the selection of suitable light waves to reveal unseen images of the microscopic universe in its living, vibrant energy state. These images can also show various forms of blockages and negative thought forms – more about this later.

He has lectured at international science conferences. In 2006, Harry gave a keynote speech at ISSSEEM, The International Society for the Study of Subtle Energies and Energy Medicine, in Boulder Colorado. Harry was later awarded the 2006 Alyce and Elmer Green Award for Innovation. (Elmer Green was the first president of the Society.)

Thought forms in the aura
Negativity is also held within the aura; evidently, thought forms appear within the emotional and mental field of our aura. Fear is that same

thought form and is there to be received by a tuned in receiver – even if that receiver has anarchy on his mind. Understanding this process and recognizing the feeling of fear is the first step to controlling it and accepting it.

When your mind accepts what it is that you fear and you face up to it, you can begin to transmute this negative thought process into useful energy that can be used as a weapon. For instance, let's say that you are too frightened to be alone in your own home. The fear you exude makes you an easier target. Your would-be attacker picks up on this negative energy and you are at risk of becoming a victim of terror. Imagine walking along a street at night, and you begin to sense negative energy. Your mind multiplies this a thousand times and creates a terrible fear. This is manifested in your mind and you exude that fear in your aura. The physical body then starts to display the body language of a fearful individual. Now you are a target for attackers. What you fear is attracted to you. The attacker is consumed with negative energy and is attracted to the source of similar energy – the principle of cause-and-effect.

Dr Barbara Brennan explains in her book how she can perceive various types of thought forms within the aura and how the color and shape of the aura shows a particular emotion. She also says there is a continuous transference between auric fields from person-to-person without the individual's knowledge. We send out these emotional signals without knowing that it happens and people then respond to the appropriate signal with no conscious knowing. Like attracts like through this magnetic attraction.

I asked the world-renowned spiritual teacher and author, William Bloom: "Imagine the thought forms that are held within your emotional field. Do you think the fear that is induced by negative thought forms could in fact act as a radio receiver to individuals with a negative disposition, and therefore attract negative experiences – very much like the law of attraction?"

He replied: *"Absolutely so, it's not so much attraction as harmonic resonance.*" He explained that your fears, aggression and negativity connects you with THE fears, aggression and negativity. Your benevolence and love connects you to THE benevolence and love.

Trust your instincts. **If it doesn't feel right, it probably isn't right. Listen to your inner voice and your in-built guidance system. This is a basic Ninja principle.**

12: MAINTAINING YOUR PERSONAL SPACE

Our personal space is an important factor in life. If someone encroaches on our space at home or in the workplace, we feel violated, and that can be a simple action such as disturbing something in your home or removing something from your desk. This violation is only lifted if we have given the permission for someone to enter our personal space.

This concept applies especially in martial arts, where you are taught to maintain your personal space and keep a safe distance between you and any potential threat. When someone breaches your personal space, you immediately feel under threat, and take the necessary precautions to protect yourself. If someone comes too close you have an overwhelming sense of encroachment and possibly fear because of the energy overlap from the other person's aura into yours, especially if the incoming energy is denser and more negative.

Everyone has an auric field, and the attributes of this field are obvious from a spiritual and psychic point of view. Each of us can use this ethereal body as a fearsome weapon – we can enhance our ability to sense and use the information contained within it. By learning to heighten your natural ability, you become more perceptible to the subtle energies that surround you. If you are a potential target, you can learn to anticipate any probable threats or impending danger.

"Your own early warning system will keep you alive."
This energy field surrounds your physical being in every way and is commonly known as your auric field. It consists of the physical, emotional, mental and etheric, or spiritual, bodies. Within this field is every thought and emotion your body exudes, the blueprint of your life-plan for past, present and future. Its colors change with different emotions

or physical expressions. It is scientific fact the auric field exists – revealed through photographic evidence by Semyon Davidovich Kirlian in 1939 – and learning to read this subtle energy puts you in an advantageous position.

Rings of protection

Let's look at the make up of the aura and how it can aid us in protecting our mind, body and spirit. From my years of training as a bodyguard, I learned that protection was much like an onion whose layers denote the concentric rings of protection. The aura is also made up of many layers of protection:

Etheric – This is the first layer that most psychically gifted individuals can see. It extends approx half an inch from the body and almost acts as a second skin. Within this layer, physical ailments can be detected. It looks silvery blue in color though some see the color as gray. This layer also holds the blueprint of your physical body.

Emotional – This layer contains the emotions you are feeling at any moment, so the colors within the aura can change according to how you are feeling. How can this emotional state effect the ability to look after your mind, body and spirit? If you are feeling the emotion of fear, then you will exude that emotion and any sensitive individuals would be able to pick up that emotion. It also exudes the emotion that we feel for others outside ourselves – so if you are feeling anger at someone then that emotion would be easily recognizable. This can be an early warning sign to you if you learn how to recognize the emotional state of others.

Mental – The mental layer contains the information on your beliefs, intellect and personal power relating to the sum total of who you are in the physical and mental sense. The thought processes are registered in this area – your decisions in what you think are registered in this field. The color of this field is mainly yellow and thought forms are structured as unshapely blobs of energy. The thought forms that are in our awareness at the time are registered in this field. It is obvious that with training and raising our awareness, we can pick up on these thoughts through the sixth sense – another key to personal protection.

Imagine standing in a bus shelter. Someone approaches you and you instinctively feel uneasy – why? Have you picked up on his thoughts? The energy the person exudes is negative and he may be thinking evil thoughts – this is what you feel. Your early warning system has been activated.

Learn to read the auric field

By now, you will have an in-depth idea of the auric field and its associations to the body on all levels. Understanding how fear or negative energy reacts within the aura is the first step in learning to defend yourself utilizing your sixth sense. Aggression, like any emotional thought form, shows itself within the aura and can be an early warning signal to imminent violence. If you can pick up this negative emotional energy, then you can take the necessary precautions to remove yourself from the vicinity of danger.

We must learn how to notice these waves of thought and how we can control them. By simply noticing the thoughts and allowing them to leave our mind in a loving manner, we gain control of the emotional field that surrounds us and we gain control of our fears. To remain positive in the face of adversity shows us that we do not need to allow negative emotion to control our life.

Strengthening the aura

Remember the stronger the energy surrounding you, the stronger you will be in securing your environment – helping you to heighten your awareness to protect all that you have in mind, body and spirit.

There are many ways to ensure that your aura remains strong and impenetrable from outside forces. Meditation is by far the easiest way to strengthen your aura by your intention only. By visualizing and believing in what you are doing, you will succeed in strengthening all levels of your auric field. Visualize yourself inside a bubble of white light. To increase this light, you must breathe in deeply asking for the universe to cleanse your aura. As you breathe out, use your intention to release any negativity that is within you or surrounds you, send it back to the universe for transmuting to positive energy. As you breathe out, you will note the white energy filling your aura and making it strong and impenetrable. You must learn to visualize this in picture form and believe in what you see, "to believe is to conceive".

Intention is very simple; if I am sitting on a chair and I decide to stand up and move into the kitchen, I use my intention. Firstly, my thought is conceived in my mind – the feeling of wanting to move from the chair to the kitchen. I see this visually and then make the intent manifest to move. This is the same with any intention that you have in your life. Many years ago, I studied another martial form called Taekwondo. Part of learning this art is learning how to break blocks of wood; the first time I tried, I failed. The instructor, Dickie, recognized that I had not visualized breaking the wood and my intention was not focused on that. After a long lecture and a bit of training on visualization I took my place and did it again – this time, to success.

You have to have belief in your ability and in yourself. Believe that you can make yourself safe and you will.

When you are positive and have positive affirmations, the effect is also positive on your auric field. Your aura becomes vibrant in color, and the aura is charged with positive energy – with thought forms that are in vibrational harmony with your affirmations, and as that change is manifested, you will find that your vibration matches that of your conscious thought-process, following the law of attraction.

Learn to meditate

In today's stressful world, we need to find ways to escape from the everyday pressures of life. It is evident that stress is around us everywhere. You only need to watch the evening news to see its effects, and every one of us knows someone who has succumbed to its power. When we let these pressures build up, our health suffers as we bottle up tensions within us. We become angry and consumed by aggression and fear, which results in all types of problems, from headaches and migraines to high blood pressure and the lowering of our immune system, so we end up catching whatever virus is working its way around.

An effective route to learning how to notice and control our thought patterns is to learn how to meditate. To learn to relax, and to understand that we are the co-creators of our own destiny and have the ability to achieve anything at all.

A great friend of mine, James, who works in senior management of a large worldwide blue-chip company, uses meditation to handle the stresses of his job. The petrochemical industry is fraught with stress, and James has known of many individuals who have given up their careers because of stress. As a birthday present, his wife sent him on holiday to a Buddhist meditation camp. Just like my friend, who has managed to be successful in life by dealing with his stresses in meditative practice – you can too.

The most effective way to combat stress is meditation, for when we meditate we are able to commune at a higher vibration. At this level is the gift of knowing all there is by communing with our creating force, so solutions can be perceived more easily. Everyone who learns to meditate returns with a new-found zeal and far more energy to deal with the trials and tribulations of their environments.

Meditation is becoming widely recognized as a tool to relieve stress and to help cope with obstacles or problems, including health issues. Major corporations now bring in experts to teach their staff how to meditate. They have seen the benefits of meditation resulting in less down-time due to illness and have seen an increase in the productivity of the workforce. In Japanese culture, emphasis is placed on meditation, and the Japanese believe this is the reason for their successes. Organizations have seen the benefits in as little as four weeks of using a focused meditative exercises resulting in changes of consciousness. These positive results include higher concentration levels, improved memory, greater self-confidence and less time off sick.

Meditation is a simple art and anyone can do it, yet many of us find it beyond our reach. You just need to train your mind to focus and concentrate. Meditation can be done in any position, but I would recommend a comfortable chair away from any distractions in quiet surroundings. Make sure that you unplug the phone and you avoid anything that could jolt you or make you jump. It is a good idea to play some relaxing music as you close your eyes and get comfortable, and have a blanket in case you get cold. Start by taking a few deep breaths, inhaling and exhaling slowly, and just place your attention on your breathing at this time. You can then move your attention to different parts of your body, starting with your toes and working upwards, telling each part to relax and let go. Soon you will feel a lot calmer and ready to begin to visualize different scenes in your mind.

Meditation is the expansion of your own consciousness or raising your vibration to match the vibration of a higher spiritual plane. It is all about entering the area of quiet and cutting out the chatter of your mind to enable you to link to your higher self.

Meditate at your own pace

There are many methods of meditation, and these practices have been around for thousands of years. The ancient Samurai would meditate regularly in their gardens – practicing the art of Zen meditation. The Celtic Druids had their own form of meditation and in India much emphasis is placed on meditation principles to become one with the universe.

The forms of meditation are vast and every form has a different modality. In the Christian traditions monks meditated by praying or saying the rosary. Even to this day, the Rosary is a form of meditative prayer within the Catholic religion. In modern times, you can meditate when you take any form of exercise or when you go walking. Meditation does not have to have the label of esoteric or new age beliefs that suggest you should sit in the lotus position ohmming to yourself. In Islam, meditation is known as the salat, which is done five times a day. This is the practice of joining the heart and mind with Allah, the detailed contemplation commanded in the Quran. In Judaism, the kabbalah is a form of meditative study. The soul is said to conduct a journey in the meditative state to achieve aims and objectives.

For many years, meditation has been an integral part of religious practice, though in the present day there are no constraints of religion given to meditation, and anyone can achieve the blending of mind, body and spirit. There are certain prerequisites of meditative practices such as discouraging the use of any drugs or alcohol. These are known to induce negative states within the body and mind and are not conducive to safe practice of meditation. Any one who studies Asian martial arts will be aware that a simple requirement of the student is that they lead a life that is harmonious to a life that respects life in all shapes and forms. This leads the student to a heightened sense of awareness by blending mind, body and spirit with all elements of nature.

Meditation and positive thinking

Is there a link between meditation and positive thinking? Think about this for a while and see what you come up with. Here the answer lies in your meditation. When you meditate, you raise your vibration to mimic the vibration of the creative life force. In this state, we are able to communicate at a higher level and the side effects of normal physicality on our return are heightened awareness. Therefore, meditation is the key to life. When you want something, you contemplate on it, you believe that you are going to get it and the universe brings this into your awareness. In essence, this is a form of positive thinking. Remaining in a state of disbelief or negativity does not allow for the matching of vibration to mimic the level of vibration of the creative forces. Therefore, nothing is brought into the awareness matching your positivism – rather negatively, you attract the opposite. By remaining positive, you are able to bring to fruition your heart's desires, which are in accordance with your life's plan. A positive state of mind is also an excellent stepping-stone to entering that level of awareness that deepens your meditative ability.

Calming your mind

The problem that most of us come up against is that when we meditate and finally get to the state where we are about to make the transition to the other realm, our conscious mind gets in the way. Before I explain the mind-chatter like "when will I get the shopping or I must fix the car", let me explain the difference between the conscious mind and the subconscious mind.

The conscious mind is the thinking individual's mind. It is that part of consciousness that creates the act of thinking about your chosen subject and the part that you can control. It has the ability to perceive the relationship between oneself and one's environment. It is the process of being in the here and now – of knowing that I am here and objectively, I can choose my own relationship between mind and physical reality.

The subconscious mind is entirely different and is the relationship between the spiritual and co-creating force. It is in the knowing of all things on a deeper level that for the moment remains subjective. Individuals are not aware of the effects of conscious behavior – the relationship between psychic forces of the soul is more prevalent in this state of consciousness.

The conscious mind can inhibit the effects and ability of meditation because it allows our mind chatter to become ever more prevalent in our thoughts. The effect of one thought normally creates another thought and so the vicious circle is constant, as energy in motion. So how do we stop the mind chatter – it's not easy. Reducing the effects of mind-chatter is more a discipline that has to become a learned behavior. The first step is recognizing when you begin to have these thought processes and dealing with each one individually. In the instance that you notice a thought coming to you, like "I have to pick up the kids". You should recognize this thought and see it dissipate – do not allow your emotions to override the meditation.

The best tip I can give is to visualize the scene that you had already started with or perhaps start with a new visualization. In time, this discipline will retrain your conscious mind and you will become the master of your own thoughts – this can be likened to achieving enlightenment as noted in the Buddhist teachings.

Visualization

Everyone can learn visualization skills. It takes time and practice, but the benefits are worth it. With a positive state of mind and regular meditation, you can heal yourself from within, bringing mental, physical and emotional relief. By using visualization skills, you give your mind and brain a chance to recharge. You are basically stopping yourself from thinking about problems and stresses, so release anything negative that is presently on your mind. This could be done in many ways. In a guided meditation, you could visualize yourself climbing a hill. As you climb you will drop all your stresses and strains of life off in bags that make you lighter as you climb. You free your mind, and it is like a wonderful break for your body and mind. You can even do this by intention alone. Just having the intent to free your mind and release your worries is enough – though you must believe that it is done. Visualizing yourself lying on a lovely beach listening to the sounds of the sea and reading a good book sends signals to your brain of feeling happy and contented. This releases endorphins with a calming effect on the nervous system. You can choose whatever scene makes you happy, perhaps a walk in the country rather than lying on the beach.

The basis is that your mind at some level believes that you are there. Trying this is a safe, worthwhile and enjoyable exercise, and building up the meditation over a few weeks will soon help you to notice a difference in your life. So if you feel you are under stress or in need of a break, but you cannot find the time to get away, give yourself a chance to experience what is now becoming the medicine of the future. Always focus on what you want, not what you don't want, and watch how you change the world around you.

Shakti Gawain's book *Creative Visualization* is recommended if you want to learn to visualize. Some individuals come up to me and tell me that they cannot visualize – they do not know how to do it. My response is usually "rubbish" as I ask them to think back to a time in their childhood. Once they are there, I ask them to describe simple things such as what they were wearing that day, what they were doing. After they have gone on for half an hour telling me every little detail of the day out to the park or seaside, I say, "now tell me you can't visualize, you just did." In that instant they look like they have just seen a ghost when their own self-realization has just hit.

Exercises

Try the exercise outlined in Box 3, either with a partner or within a group of like-minded individuals.

Sensory Exercise

Meditate for at least 20 minutes. This could be a guided meditation from a CD or by listening to soft, subtle music. Like the Samurai, try to achieve the state of 'no mind'. Empty your mind of all the thoughts of the day and try to achieve a state where you see or sense your thoughts. Accept them and blow them away with your out-breath.

Begin breathing deeply, in-and-out. With every out-breath, release into the universe all the worries of the day, as well as the deeper ones that haunt your mind.

After you have completed your meditation, remain in this

---

relaxed state with your breathing controlled. Stand with your back to your partner, and put on a blindfold.

When you are ready, tell your higher self that you are tuned into the natural surroundings and all the energy it contains. With your mind in this state, remain as relaxed as possible.

When your partner is ready, he or she will move forward with a negative intent or with the thought to harm you. Your partner must adopt that mind-set and think of the worst thing possible, with the intent of using that negative force.

When you feel that emotion, or your mind picks up the negative sensation, you must move instantly. This is the experience and sensation that you feel from that energy. It is your intuitive ability warning you of danger.

The exercise meditation

For those who find meditating in the quiet difficult, try meditating while doing exercise. If you can try to enter the quiet of the exercise and begin to meditate on a creative visualization, you will be amazed at what you can achieve. Of course, you need to do this when you are not in danger of falling or tripping over something. My wife Jo finds jogging excellent for meditating, and we have predicted many future events while exercising.

I like to go training in the country, find a tranquil spot and go through my sword Katas. It has been my way of meditating – to become one with nature. The countryside is quiet and serene, my vibration raises. Whenever I have felt the need for contemplation, I have always been drawn to water, the sea or a meandering stream, to cleanse my energy field and help me to gain insights into life. It can be easier to meditate in environments like this without having to enter into any esoteric modality – meditation is life and life is meditation in the right place for mind, body and soul.

By learning to meditate, we learn to achieve a state where we can control our emotional state, and this is one of the keys in using our ability to remain safe in a hostile world. Over time, by achieving a calm and still mind, you should gain a higher percentage of success, and develop the ability to sense the subtle forces of energy, especially danger. You will be accessing your intuition and natural psychic ability.

CHAPTER 13: TRAINING YOUR SIXTH SENSE

These are a few exercises you can try to help you develop your psychic abilities. Some of the exercises may sound pointless, but if you concentrate and carry out the exercises with intent, you will be amazed at what you can achieve.

Ask for Protection

Before you attempt any psychic training, you must ask for protection because you will be opening yourself up spiritually, and therefore will become a target to mischievous spirits and or negative entities. Anyone who tells you that there is nothing to worry about, is either blind to the truth or has so much fear in them that they will not give credence to the truth that evil and negativity does exist. Therefore, we have to take precautions. Imagine what would happen if you went on to a roller coaster without any protection – you would fall out and probably be seriously injured or killed. Just as we take precautions during the ride to keep us safe, like strapping yourself in or wearing a safety belt in a car, so too do we take precautions with our own spirituality.

Ask for protection from the Christ light (the strongest form of protection) or the Holy Spirit. See the white light of the Holy Spirit surround you and create a shield of protection. You could invoke the help of Archangel Michael and ask that he places a cloak of protection around you. Another method is to imagine yourself walking into a violet flame or asking your guides to draw near and protect you. All you have to do is ask. I normally say the following prayer: *"I ask for the protection of the Christ light to surround me and protect me from all negative energies and discarnate entities that would hinder me spiritually or cause annoyance to me in any part of my life. I also ask for my guides and angels to draw*

close to me and teach me what I need to know from spirit for my highest
good and the highest good of all humankind."

For me this prayer has been an incredible prayer of protection that I
have used for a long time. If I am carrying out an exorcism or clearance,
I will invoke the protection of Archangel Michael.

"I invoke the divine protection of Michael the Archangel who is the
lord of the way and protector of all heaven and earth. Michael, please
protect and guide me for the job that needs to be done – be my guiding
light and guide and protect me with your mighty sword of truth."

The Tuning In Game

The first is a game we call the 'Tuning in Game', which starts as fun, then
becomes more serious the more adept we become. This is an exercise that
you need to do with a partner, so it would be best to find someone who is
of like mind.

Firstly, before any questions are asked, you will need to take a few
moments to meditate and tune yourself in to the psychic vibrations that
surround you. One person asks questions first, and they should be
pertinent to the other person's past. The subject and not the questioner
must then validate each answer. Practice this until you begin to have a
fairly good hit rate. The type of questions that you can ask would be:

"Did you have a doll when you were younger that had one missing eye
and a broken finger?"

If this is validated then you are picking up strong psychic vibes.
Perhaps you could ask a more mundane question about the past – for
instance:

"You visited Arizona when you were young and brought back an
Indian statue."

These may be direct statements rather than questions but if these are
validated, then you know you are getting psychic information. You could
pick up on a medical condition with the person in either the past or
present, but start with the past. If those statements are a little hard to pick

up because of the detail, start of small by saying:

"I am seeing a picture of you walking by water yesterday, can you understand this?"

If the person validates this – you are beginning to build your psychic building blocks for the future. You can then progress, as you feel fit.

After you have practiced this for a notable time and you are beginning to get a little better, buy yourself a psychic vibes journal. This journal is where you will start to note down your vibes. Jo and I have a few that we use for different things. Sometimes, we will use the journal to tune into our future and then write down the answers.

See your forecast

Take a little time to tune into your vibes; perhaps you and your partner could have a meditation for five or ten minutes. Ask the universe to show you what is in store for you in the next two weeks and write down every-thing you get in your journal, no matter how trivial it may seem. Write down how you received the information and what form. For instance, you may have seen a picture in your mind or you may have heard the words in your mind, this means that you are working clairvoyantly or clairaudi-ently. As the two weeks unfold, you will find out if you are right or wrong.

What's in the envelope?

Another great game that my wife and I do on a regular basis with our students is to choose individual photographs and place them in sealed envelopes. We get each of the students to meditate for a little while - whilst holding the sealed envelope. They then have to tune into the vibration surrounding the envelope and then write down on a blank piece of paper everything they are receiving in their minds eye. It could be that one person see's water or a river or a color or something as simple as that.

As before, the student will be marked on the number of hits they manage to achieve. Clearly, your vibes will become stronger the more you practice and you will be able to identify more things with far more information and precision.

Where are you?

You have come across the phenomena of remote viewing in earlier chapters. This game is fun and can keep you occupied for hours – it is remote viewing in its basic form. One of you needs to take a short drive somewhere, a walk, or public transport to an area that is unknown to your partner. Once you have reached the destination you have chosen, you need to let your partner know that you have arrived by sending a text to their cell phone or other arranged sign. Be sure the sign does not give the location away; do not call them as you can tell the location by sounds that are audible. The other person who has remained at the base location must now meditate for ten minutes and ask to be shown where your partner is. What can you see in the immediate vicinity, is it shops, is it a river? Maybe they are standing in the woods. Getting any small piece of information that can be validated is an excellent beginning to developing your remote viewing ability.

Blind Man's Bluff

I have always had natural abilities but I was an ad hoc medium that did readings for people without proper platform training. After my father's passing, I had no idea how to use them properly, so I decided to get that training. It was the hardest course I had ever done. Jo was a hard teacher; she made us do a blind reading and double-blind reading. You can do this too though you need volunteers who are open-minded. One person has to stay in a room, blindfolded and the controller overseeing the test chooses someone from another room to come forward. This must be in total silence. When you are all in place, allow the blinded person to tune in for a short time and then ask some questions:

- Is the individual in a relationship and what type?
- Do they have children?
- What is their job?
- What did they do yesterday?
- What is the medical condition of the person?
- Give the name of a person that is close to them in the family?

The questions must be scored in relevance to their truth, and there are to be no half measures. You need the job title or as close as you can get to the type of work. Remember there are no absolutes and the universe will show you signs – do not miss them. You will be amazed at what you can receive and you will do well to get two or three right first time round.

ESP and Telepathy

Everyone has heard about the extra sensory perception tests (ESP) with cards that have shapes on them like a star, triangle, circle and wavy lines. The scientist sits in front of the subject and asks them to say what card he is looking at – he scores the number of direct hits the subject has. We developed our own method that is a lot more fun and helps to develop your telepathy skills.

One of you sends the thought and the other receives it, whatever comes. The sender chooses an image or a word to send – you concentrate on the object or word, see it in your mind and visualize sending it to your partner. The partner needs to wait, empty the mind and think of nothing. Ask the universe for protection and to be shown what is being sent. Now write down what comes into your mind instantaneously.

You can choose anything at all as long as the thought has the vibration of a higher level. If you think about negative thoughts and send negative thoughts – you will open a 'Pandora's box' of problems.

Try this exercise. Send your partner to the shops and do not tell then what you want. Do not give them any particular amount of money and ask them just to walk about the area. Send the telepathic message and buy whatever comes to your mind. Jo and I always do this and 90 per cent of the time, we are successful.

Psychometry

Psychometry is the ability to read the energy imprint of an animate (living) or inanimate (non-living) object just as we tune in and read our auras. 'Psyche' means soul and 'metry' means meter to measure, which means the reading of auras around objects and people. I discussed in a previous chapter about our energy field, the pioneering work of Harry Oldfield and the fact that energy remains imprinted on any object that would be exposed to, particularly strong energy that surrounds both types of energy fields.

The auric fields of people, animals, trees, plants and flowers, has a far greater energy than that of places and objects such as old buildings, jewelery and furniture. Psychometry proves that everything we do, think and say is all around and a part of us. Psychometry is the reading of the past and present conditions of the person, place or object and can be used to help gain a link to the spirit world.

Jo and I have much fun with this especially when we are out and about. It is great to practice in old buildings like castles and other antiquated buildings. All you really need do is touch or feel the object and tune into its vibration, soon images and impressions will come to your mind.

I once went into a castle in the north of Scotland, my cousin let slip that I was a medium and as I walked around the building I began to receive very vivid psychic impressions. Soon afterwards, I had a few of the staff walking around with me testing my ability. One particular room had a large four-poster bed, and as I held on to one of the posts, I received incredibly vivid images. I saw a rape and a servant woman who was taken by the head of the house. I also saw that the woman had an illegitimate child and was dealt with. One of the members of staff was amazed by this revelation and introduced me to the castle's curator, who told me the information I had was accurate. Skeptics would refute this and say that I could have already known, but this information was not known to any but the curator and the staff and was not in the public domain.

Current and Future Events

One exercise that my wife and I like to do is try to tune into world events in the immediate future or further in the future. When we watch events on the news that involve murders or missing persons, we normally try to tune into the proceedings and write down the feelings and visions we receive. We often manage to tune into some evidence that is relevant to the event. If you cast your mind back to the previous chapters, you will note that I successfully tuned into the military coup in Thailand and William Bloom successfully picked up on the universal vibes that warned him of the tsunami.

The above exercises are only to help you develop your gifts so you may learn to live as a sixth sensory individual in a world that is fraught with turmoil and disaster. By developing your gifts, you will be able to discern between positive and negative energies – identifying whether or not you are under psychic attack or you are being bombarded by influential energy. By becoming a sixth sensory individual, you will be able to pick up negative vibrations and thus save your life in more ways than one.

Psychokinesis – the shield

Psychokinesis is the relationship between mind and matter interactions, it's the ability for the energy to affect a material object. In Dale Graff's, book *Tracks in the Psychic Wilderness* he talks about one of his subjects called Dianne who experienced phenomena like this since childhood. Intelligence agencies throughout the world have been studying this mind, matter interaction to discover its lethal potential. So far, nothing has been documented that suggests that psychokinesis can be used negatively. An interesting point to note is that in some Japanese Budo traditions – psychokinesis is apparent as a normal part of the art. The person who has developed his or her skills to an extremely high level is able to affect the electro-muscular contractions of the opponent by manipulating energy alone. Psychokinetic energy is inherent in most Japanese martial arts, even though many individuals do not recognize it as such. It is possible to train oneself in learning to manipulate the Ki to affect the materialistic nature of an object or a human. Perhaps as science evolves, we will be able to understand that energy and put it to a far superior productive use. We can stop an attacker dead in his tracks by intention of that psychokinetic energy alone.

14: CONCLUSION

The Path of a Warrior

In ancient times, a warrior tried to live his life in harmony with the universe and to understand what path he must travel. Along the road, he would have encountered many hardships and trials, but he would never succumb to these vicissitudes. Instead, he used them to develop his own Budo path even further.

In everyday life, our actions will also show the warrior paths, and the actions we take denote the truth in our lives. In order to teach we must understand; in order to understand we must feel; and in order to feel we must trial and live. These are my thoughts on warrior values. Throughout my life as a warrior and an exponent of true Budo, I have followed many paths and witnessed many lives being destroyed. Reflecting on these experiences has strengthened my understanding of my own Budo path. I believe in the preservation of life, and yet in order to preserve the lives that I protected, I have had to face the demons that would destroy them. I have looked into the mouth of the dragon (death) on three occasions, and each time my strength and belief in Budo has brought me back from that barren wasteland and mouth of eternal destruction.

A true warrior understands the control he must exercise to show the qualities of mercy appropriate for a ninja or samurai. In combat, you have the chance to look into the eyes of your enemy and almost touch their souls. You have the ability to neutralize, but by showing mercy, you start on a new path of enlightenment, and so the path of Budo becomes more meaningful. To learn to forgive even the demon reveals a true warrior.

There may come a point when you must neutralize the threat, and how you choose to do this reflects your own spirituality. In the service and protection of others, one can argue that this is a necessary evil. Your martial path has now touched the elements of truth and distinguishes between those holy places of heaven and hell. Without them, there would be no balance, no yin and yang, no understanding and no opportunity to better oneself through absorbing moral values. Although your parents will have taught you moral values, you have the freedom and free will to endure hardships that cleanse your spirit and to find your own Budo path.

This is one element of life that you must choose for yourself.

I have written this book to give you an insight in how to protect yourself and your family through learning to use your sixth sense. The book contains hints and tips that will allow your mind to open to new sources and forms of information. I hope that it makes a practical contribution to help you gain a wider understanding and knowledge. You should have enhanced your ability to protect yourself in all circumstances and now rely on prevention rather than cure.

I hope that you will keep this book with you and use it often. Just browsing through now and again should give you hope and further understanding, and it may usefully jog your memory about simple techniques you can use to increase your level of security in mind, body and spirit.

What does it mean to live in a sixth-sensory world? Living with your sixth sense allows you to detect subtle imbalances in fields of energy. Everything exists as energy, even if perceived as a solid form. By attuning yourself to this frequency, you will be able to identify, perceive and anticipate possible problems that may manifest in life, from street-level violence to international incidents by terrorists. As a sixth-sensory security specialist, you will become a true bodyguard of the self and the environment, making the world a safer place.

APPENDIX: SCIENTIFIC VIEWS

The Sense of Being Stared At
by Rupert Sheldrake

In his latest book, biologist Rupert Sheldrake explores the intricacies of the mind and discovers that our perceptive abilities are stronger than many of us could have imagined. Most of us know it well – the almost physical sensation that we are the object of someone's attention. And what about related phenomena, such as telepathy and premonitions? Are they merely subjective beliefs? Basing his conclusions on years of intense research, Sheldrake argues persuasively that such phenomena are real.

Seven Experiments That Could Change the World:
A Do-It-Yourself Guide to Revolutionary Science
by Rupert Sheldrake

Rupert Sheldrake's groundbreaking book examines unexplained natural phenomena and suggests explanations that push the boundaries of science. How does your pet know when you are coming home? How do pigeons home? Can people really feel a "phantom" amputated arm? These questions and more form the basis of Sheldrake's look at the world of contemporary science as he puts some of the most cherished assumptions of established science to the test. Sheldrake's website allows anyone to take part in ongoing experiments.

Dr Dean Radin is Laboratory Director at the Institute of Noetic Sciences, founded in 1973 by Apollo 14 astronaut, Dr Edgar Mitchell. CRL focuses on laboratory studies of mind-matter interaction, clairvoyance, precognition, distant healing, and other forms of anomalous perception and action. CRL has also investigated reportedly haunted sites, persons claiming exceptional psychic abilities, and environmental and possible psi-related factors associated with games of chance.

Dr Radin's research is one of the most detailed that I have come across; he has stunned me with his research into senses beyond our physical 5. His new book that was released this year: 2006, is an exhaustive account of the research that has been carried out to date. (Entangled Minds; Paraview Pocket Books 2006). Below is an excerpt from the first chapter of his first book (The Conscious Universe) that epitomizes psychic phenomena

.http://www.deanradin.com/default_original.html
The Conscious Universe by Dean Radin
Excerpt from Chapter 1
The idea is that those compelling, perplexing and sometimes profound human experiences known as "psychic phenomena" are real. The reality of psychic phenomena is now no longer based solely upon faith, or wishful thinking, or absorbing anecdotes. It is not even based upon the results of a few scientific experiments. We know that these phenomena exist because of new ways of evaluating massive amounts of scientific evidence collected over a century by scores of researchers.

Psychic, or "psi" phenomena fall into two general categories. The first is perception of objects or events beyond the range of the ordinary senses. The second is mentally causing action at a distance. In both categories, it seems that intention, the mind's will, can do things that – according to prevailing scientific theories – it isn't supposed to be able to do. We wish to know what is happening to loved ones, and somehow, sometimes, that information is available, even over large distances. Mind willing, many interesting things appear to be possible.

Understanding such experiences requires an expanded view of human consciousness. Is the mind merely a mechanistic, information-processing bundle of neurons? Is it a "computer made of meat" as some cognitive scientists and neuroscientists believe? Or is it something more? The evidence suggests that while many aspects of mental functioning are undoubtedly related to brain structure and electrochemical activity, there is also something else happening, something very interesting.

Psi has been shown to exist in thousands of experiments... the fact is that virtually all scientists who have studied the evidence, including the hard-nosed skeptics, now agree that there is something interesting going on that merits serious scientific attention.

The Cognitive Research Laboratory (CRL)

The Cognitive Science Laboratory, has been the home of the US Governments investigations into Extra Sensory Perception (ESP) since 1985. It is also the home of the much publicized project STARGATE. The project was funded mainly by the government and cost in excess of 20 million dollars until the closure of the program in 1995. It is now funded exclusively by private means and continues the research to this day. Now in it's twentieth year, it has been a hive of activity in the parapsychology field and has conducted thousands of research tests to prove the existence and usage of ESP and other psychic phenomena. Its primary goal was to investigate such things as precognition, clairvoyance, remote viewing and psycho kinesis. Below I have detailed the mission statement of the CSL.

The mission of the Cognitive Sciences Laboratory is three-fold: to use the tools of modern behavioral, physiological, and physical sciences to:

Determine which parapsychological phenomena can be validated under strict laboratory conditions.

Understand their mechanisms.

Examine the degree to which they might contribute to practical applications.

The laboratory is a center for interdisciplinary research devoted to understanding a wide range of human experience. In addition to exploring Para psychological phenomena, the Cognitive Sciences Laboratory's charter extends to allied fields such as consciousness research, cognitive neuroscience, perception, physiology, psychology and physics. http://www.lfr.org/LFR/csl/index.html

You can note from the above statement that the CSL has been actively involved in experimentation of psychic phenomena and even now in 2006 and 2007, you can get involved in their continuing experimentation.

There is no doubting it, the more we expand the understanding of human consciousness, the more we will seek further answers. From the time when no one believed we could ever communicate by any other means than speech – we now have the internet that lives in a consciousness of its own. We also have mobile communications that have evolved from Alexander Graham Bell's own invention – the telephone. We have moved in leaps and bounds and achieved an understanding of the impossible and now scientists are expanding that consciousness with further experimentation.

For many years, Government intelligence agencies have experimented with psychic phenomena. They have used psychics, Scientists and experts of the mind to further their advances in the fight against crime and terrorism. Every experiment done has been top secret until now and the scientists involved have remained silent until now. One famous investigation was that of project STARGATE – the American Army's investigation into remote viewing.

One of the main operatives in this project was Joseph McMoneagle, author of *The Remote Viewing Handbook*, Hampton Roads 2000. He was subjected to rigorous testing in the laboratory along with other individuals that had psychic abilities. Joseph spent almost 15 years at the Cognitive Science Lab (CSL) as a research associate and subject. He worked in an operational capacity until the closure of Project STARGATE in 1995. It is important to note that no Government agency would throw resources into an operation of this sort had the scientific evidence not been there to warrant it. Dale E. Graff, was a former director of project STARGATE and a Physicist whose scientific research has evolved into various best selling books.

http://www.dalegraff.com/

Dale E. Graff, facilitator and author, is a physicist and a former director of project STARGATE, the government program that investigated remote viewing phenomena.

River Dreams expands the theme of psychic exploration introduced by *Tracks in the Psychic Wilderness*. It has many examples of psi phenomena, or extrasensory perception (ESP) from the author's personal experiences, from Para psychological research and from operational projects in the government's STARGATE program. *River Dreams* focuses on psi in the dream state, although psi experienced in the conscious state, such as via intuition and remote viewing are central aspects of the various episodes described. Specific incidents are written in a first person style to capture the sense of discovery, and to illustrate the motivation and meaning aspects of the circumstances.

A comment from Maj Gen E R Thompson, US Army Assistant Chief of Staff for Intelligence (1977-81)

"My own involvement with remote viewing was to learn to improve its accuracy and reliability for real-world operational applications. I left it to the scientists to explain how it works. Dale Graff, both an operational practitioner and a scientist, provides a well-reasoned approach for using and understanding psychic phenomena."

There is no doubting that Dale Graff is a scientist in the forefront of paranormal research or normal research if you want to coin a phrase. His experiments are a deciding factor on the validity of the expansion of human consciousness – anyone who wants hard evidence should study his books to gain further insight.

Energy and information
Consider this, if you look at a solid object, what does it seem to you? When you touch it, it feels solid; to move it, you would have to exert some other point of energy upon it. However, what if I told you that what you are looking at is an illusion, in fact everything that seems solid, does not really exist as that solid matter. Solid matter is just made up of atoms that vibrate at a very high frequency; they bind and cause us to perceive

them as solid objects. Everything that surrounds us in life is energy in motion; therefore, we are all energy in motion too. Every living cell that we have in our bodies is in fact energy in motion and therefore an illusion of our perception. World-renowned scientists epitomize this in the following statements:

> *"It seems probable to me that God in the beginning formed matter in solid, massy, hard, impenetrable, movable particles, of such sizes and figures, and with such other properties, and in such proportion to space, as most conduced to the end for which he formed them. These primitive particles being solids, are incomparably harder than any porous bodies compounded of them; even so very hard, as never to wear or break in pieces; no ordinary power being able to divide what God himself made one in the first creation." (**Newton**, From 'The Tao of Physics', p64)*

> *According to general relativity, the concept of space detached from any physical content (matter, objects) does not exist. The physical reality of space is represented by a field whose components are continuous functions of four independent variables - the co-ordinates of space and time. Since the theory of general relatively implies the representation of physical reality by a continuous field, the concept of* ***particles*** *or material points cannot play a fundamental part, nor can the concept of motion. The particle can only appear as a limited region in space in which the field strength or the energy densities are particularly high. (Einstein, 1954)*

It is important to note the atoms to which we are referring are of an indestructible nature, and therefore whatever happens to the matter, such as physical death – the body just breaks into those atoms and other particles. Therefore, we exist as energy in motion.

Would it then be reasonable to assume that if everything is as we have deduced, we should be able to manipulate that matter to identify our reasons for existence or there may be a guiding universal force. Should we not be able to tune into that vibration to gain answers to the questions we have within us.

BIBLIOGRAPHY

Sources Used

Materials were drawn from several websites:

Official website of the UK Security Service, www.MI5.gov.uk

10 Downing Street www.pm.gov.uk

Jane's Information Group www.janes.com

Criminal Statistics, www.crimestatistics.org

Foreign and Commonwealth Office, www.fco.gov.uk

National Online Resource Centre on Violence Against Women, www.vawnet.org

Hidden Hurt, Abuse Information and Support Site, www.hiddenhurt.co.uk

Books, journals and other sources used:

Reports by Self-Defense Governing Body, incorporated under Statutory Instrument 1685

Kroll Associates Studies

Criminal Law Act 1967

Assaults - Offences against the Person Act 1861

The Guardian newspaper

The Art of War by Sun Tzu

Kidnap, Hijack, Siege, A Control Risks Publication, 1998

Metropolitan Police Newsletter, 2003

The Bodyguard Manual by J Tombs

The Essence of Ninjutsu: The Nine Traditions by Maasaki Hatsumi, 1988

The Psychic in You by Jeffrey A Wands, 2005

Picture Perfect, the Medicine of the Future by Joanne Pugsley, 2005

The Conscious Universe by Dean Radin (Harper Collins 1997)

Tracks in the Psychic Wilderness by Dale E. Graff (Vega 1998)

A Little Light On Spiritual Laws by Diana Cooper (Hodder Mobius)

The Sense of Being Stared At by Rupert Sheldrake (Arrow 2004)

Practical Psychic Self-Defense by Robert Bruce (Hampton Roads 2002)

Creative Visualization and Meditation Exercises to Enrich Your Life by Shakti Gawain (New World Library, 1997)

Veritas.arizona.edu Veritas research programme

NOTES

1 *The Essence of Ninjutsu: The Nine Traditions* by Maasaki Hatsumi, published 1988.

2 Kroll Assocates Study 1995

3 CRG Kidnap Hijack Seige How to Survive as Hostage 1989

4 Kroll Associates Study, 2003.

5 British Self-Defense Governing Body, incorporated under Statutory Instrument 1685

6 Assaults - Offences against the Person Act 1861

7 Self-Defence Governing Body, incorporated under Statutory Instrument 1685, Criminal Law Act 1967.

8 *The Guardian* newspaper.

9 Criminal Law Act, 1967 section 3.

10 Ken Ju Ropo, Jin Ryaku no Maaki, part of transcripts of Ninjutsu.

11 The Holly Bible New Testament

12 www.hiddenhurt.com

13 National Online Resource Centre on Violence Against Women

14 This section summarizes material published on the Internet, 'Through a Rapist's Eyes' *Metropolitan Police Newsletter*, 2003

15 Boaz Gonar, *Defining Terrorism*, 2004.

16 Sources www.pm.gov.uk and www.janes.com

17 Sources www.pm.gov.uk and www.Janes.com

18 From statistical information collated by the security services.

19 Wikepedia

BOOKS

O is a symbol of the world, of oneness and unity. In different cultures it also means the "eye," symbolizing knowledge and insight. We aim to publish books that are accessible, constructive and that challenge accepted opinion, both that of academia and the "moral majority."

Our books are available in all good English language bookstores worldwide. If you don't see the book on the shelves ask the bookstore to order it for you, quoting the ISBN number and title. Alternatively you can order online (all major online retail sites carry our titles) or contact the distributor in the relevant country, listed on the copyright page.

See our website **www.o-books.net** for a full list of over 500 titles, growing by 100 a year.

And tune in to myspiritradio.com for our book review radio show, hosted by June-Elleni Laine, where you can listen to the authors discussing their books.

MySpiritRadio

RECENT O BOOKS

Back to the Truth
5,000 years of Advaita
Dennis Waite

A wonderful book. Encyclopedic in nature, and destined to become a classic. **James Braha**

Absolutely brilliant...an ease of writing with a water-tight argument outlining the great universal truths. This book will become a modern classic. A milestone in the history of Advaita. **Paula Marvelly**
1905047614 500pp **£19.95 $29.95**

Beyond Photography
Encounters with orbs, angels and mysterious light forms
Katie Hall and John Pickering

The authors invite you to join them on a fascinating quest; a voyage of discovery into the nature of a phenomenon, manifestations of which are shown as being historical and global as well as contemporary and intently personal.

At journey's end you may find yourself a believer, a doubter or simply an intrigued wonderer... Whatever the outcome, the process of journeying is likely prove provocative and stimulating and - as with the mysterious images fleetingly captured by the authors' cameras - inspiring and potentially enlightening. **Brian Sibley**, author and broadcaster.
1905047908 272pp 50 b/w photos +8pp colour insert **£12.99 $24.95**

Don't Get MAD Get Wise
Why no one ever makes you angry, ever!
Mike George

There is a journey we all need to make, from anger, to peace, to forgiveness. Anger always destroys, peace always restores, and forgiveness always heals. This explains the journey, the steps you can take to make it happen for you.
1905047827 160pp **£7.99 $14.95**

IF You Fall...
It's a new beginning
Karen Darke

Karen Darke's story is about the indomitability of spirit, from one of life's cruel vagaries of fortune to what is insight and inspiration. She has overcome the limitations of paralysis and discovered a life of challenge and adventure that many of us only dream about. It is all about the mind, the spirit and the desire that some of us find, but which all of us possess.
Joe Simpson, mountaineer and author of *Touching the Void*
1905047886 240pp £9.99 $19.95

Love, Healing and Happiness
Spiritual wisdom for a post-secular era
Larry Culliford

This will become a classic book on spirituality. It is immensely practical and grounded. It mirrors the author's compassion and lays the foundation for a higher understanding of human suffering and hope.
Reinhard Kowalski Consultant Clinical Psychologist
1905047916 304pp **£10.99 $19.95**

A Map to God
Awakening Spiritual Integrity
Susie Anthony

This describes an ancient hermetic pathway, representing a golden thread running through many traditions, which offers all we need to understand and do to actually become our best selves.
1846940443 260pp £10.99 $21.95

Punk Science
Inside the mind of God
Manjir Samanta-Laughton

Wow! Punk Science is an extraordinary journey from the microcosm of the atom to the macrocosm of the Universe and all stops in between. Manjir Samanta-Laughton's synthesis of cosmology and consciousness is sheer genius. It is elegant, simple and, as an added bonus, makes great reading.
Dr Bruce H. Lipton, author of *The Biology of Belief*
1905047932 320pp £12.95 $22.95

Rosslyn Revealed
A secret library in stone
Alan Butler

Rosslyn Revealed gets to the bottom of the mystery of the chapel featured in the Da Vinci Code. The results of a lifetime of careful research and study demonstrate that truth really is stranger than fiction; a library of philosophical ideas and mystery rites, that were heresy in their time, have been disguised in the extraordinarily elaborate stone carvings.
1905047924 260pp b/w + colour illustrations £19.95 $29.95 cl

The Way of Thomas
Nine Insights for Enlightened Living from the Secret Sayings of Jesus
John R. Mabry

What is the real story of early Christianity? Can we find a Jesus that is relevant as a spiritual guide for people today?

These and many other questions are addressed in this popular presentation of the teachings of this mystical Christian text. Includes a reader-friendly version of the gospel.
1846940303 196pp **£10.99 $19.95**

The Way Things Are
A Living Approach to Buddhism
Lama Ole Nydahl

An up-to-date and revised edition of a seminal work in the Diamond Way Buddhist tradition (three times the original length), that makes the timeless wisdom of Buddhism accessible to western audiences. Lama Ole has established more than 450 centres in 43 countries.
1846940427 240pp **£9.99 $19.95**

The 7 Ahas! of Highly Enlightened Souls
How to free yourself from ALL forms of stress
Mike George

7th printing
A very profound, self empowering book. Each page bursting with wisdom and insight. One you will need to read and reread over and over again! Paradigm Shift. I totally love this book, a wonderful nugget of inspiration.
PlanetStarz
1903816319 128pp 190/135mm **£5.99 $11.95**

God Calling
A Devotional Diary
A. J. Russell

46th printing
"When supply seems to have failed, you must know that it has not done so. But you must look around to see what you can give away. Give away something." One of the best-selling devotional books of all time, with over 6 million copies sold.
1905047428 280pp 135/95mm **£7.99** cl.
US rights sold

The Goddess, the Grail and the Lodge
The Da Vinci code and the real origins of religion
Alan Butler

5th printing
This book rings through with the integrity of sharing time-honoured revelations. As a historical detective, following a golden thread from the great Megalithic cultures, Alan Butler vividly presents a compelling picture of the fight for life of a great secret and one that we simply can't afford to ignore.
Lynn Picknett & Clive Prince
1903816696 360pp 230/152mm **£12.99 $19.95**

The Heart of Tantric Sex
A unique guide to love and sexual fulfilment
Diana Richardson

3rd printing
The art of keeping love fresh and new long after the honeymoon is over.

Tantra for modern Western lovers adapted in a practical, refreshing and sympathetic way.

One of the most revolutionary books on sexuality ever written.
Ruth Ostrow, News Ltd.
1903816378 256pp **£9.99 $14.95**

I Am With You
The best-selling modern inspirational classic
John Woolley

14th printing hardback
Will bring peace and consolation to all who read it. **Cardinal Cormac Murphy-O'Connor**
0853053413 280pp 150x100mm **£9.99** cl
4th printing paperback
1903816998 280pp 150/100mm **£6.99 $12.95**

In the Light of Meditation
The art and practice of meditation in 10 lessons
Mike George

2nd printing
A classy book. A gentle yet satisfying pace and is beautifully illustrated. Complete with a CD or guided meditation commentaries, this is a true gem among meditation guides. **Brainwave**

In-depth approach, accessible and clearly written, a convincing map of the overall territory and a practical path for the journey. **The Light**
1903816610 224pp 235/165mm full colour throughout +CD **£11.99 $19.95**

The Instant Astrologer
A revolutionary new book and software package for the astrological seeker
Lyn Birkbeck

2nd printing
The brilliant Lyn Birkbeck's new book and CD package, The Instant Astrologer, combines modern technology and the wisdom of the ancients, creating an invitation to enlightenment for the masses, just when we need it most! Astrologer **Jenny Lynch**, Host of NYC's StarPower Astrology Television Show
1903816491 628pp full colour throughout with CD ROM 240/180 **£39 $69** cl

Is There An Afterlife?
A comprehensive overview of the evidence, from east and west
David Fontana

2nd printing
An extensive, authoritative and detailed survey of the best of the evidence supporting survival after death. It will surely become a classic not only of parapsychology literature in general but also of survival literature in particular. **Universalist**
1903816904 496pp 230/153mm **£14.99 $24.95**

The Reiki Sourcebook
Bronwen and Frans Stiene

5th printing
It captures everything a Reiki practitioner will ever need to know about the ancient art. This book is hailed by most Reiki professionals as the best guide to Reiki. For an average reader, it's also highly enjoyable and a good

way to learn to understand Buddhism, therapy and healing.
Michelle Bakar, Beauty magazine
1903816556 384pp **£12.99 $19.95**

Soul Power
The transformation that happens when you know
Nikki de Carteret

4th printing
One of the finest books in its genre today. Using scenes from her own life and growth, Nikki de Carteret weaves wisdom about soul growth and the power of love and transcendent wisdom gleaned from the writings of the mystics. This is a book that I will read gain and again as a reference for my own soul growth. **Barnes and Noble review**
190381636X 240pp **£9.99 $15.95**

The Art of Being Psychic
The power to free the artist within
June Elleni-Laine

A brilliant book for anyone wishing to develop their intuition, creativity and psychic ability. It is truly wonderful, one of the best books on psychic development that I have read. I have no hesitation in recommending this book, a must for every bookshelf. **Suzanna McInerney**, former President, College of Psychic Studies
1905047541 160pp **£12.99 $24.95**

Journey Home

A true story of time and inter-dimensional travel

Tonika Rinar

2nd printing

A lifeline that has been tossed out from the universe to help tether those lost in the wake of recent world events. If you are willing to open your mind, Tonika will take you on a journey home, to a place that shines bright within each of us...... all you have to do is reach for it. **Amazon**

1905047002 272pp £11.99 $16.95

Spirit Release

A practical handbook

Sue Allen

A comprehensive and definitive guide to psychic attack, curses, witchcraft, spirit attachment, possession, soul retrieval, haunting, soul rescue, deliverance and exorcism, and more. This book is the most comprehensive I have seen on the subject of spirit release. This book is a must for anyone working and dealing with people. **Becky Walsh**, presenter of The Psychic Show on LBC

1846940338 256pp **£11.99 $24.95**

Spiritwalking

Poppy Palin

Drawing together the wild craft of the shamanic practitioner and the wise counsel of the medium or psychic, Spiritwalking takes the reader through a practical course in becoming an effective, empathic spiritwalker. In an era blighted by professional mystics, Poppy Palin is the real thing. You can

trust her - and what she writes - completely. **Alan Richardson**, author of
The Inner Guide to Egypt and others
1846940311 320pp **£11.99 $24.95**

The 9 Dimensions of the Soul
Essence and the Enneagram
David Hey

*The first book to relate the two, understanding the personality types of the
Enneagram in relation to the Essence, shedding a new light on our personality, its origins and how it operates. Written in a beautifully simple,
insightful and heartful way and transmits complex material in a way that is
easy to read and understand.* **Thomas O. Trobe**, Founder and Director of
Learning Love Seminars, Inc.
1846940028 176pp **£10.99 $19.95**

Aim for the Stars...Reach the Moon
How to coach your life to spiritual and material success
Conor Patterson

*A fascinating, intelligent, and beneficial tool and method of programming
your mind for success. The techniques are fast to achieve, motivating, and
inspiring. I highly recommend this book.* **Uri Geller**
1905047274 208pp £11.99 $19.95

Developing Spiritual Intelligence
The power of you
Altazar Rossiter

*This beautifully clear and fascinating book is an incredibly simple guide to
that which so many of us search for.* **Dr Dina Glouberman**
1905047649 240pp **£12.99 $19.95**